Hard Press

Introduction, by Neil Parsons

"Native Life in South Africa" is one of the most remarkable books on Africa, by one of the continent's most remarkable writers. It was written as a work of impassioned political propaganda, exposing the plight of black South Africans under the whites-only government of newly unified South Africa. It focuses on the effects of the 1913 Natives' Land Act which introduced a uniform system of land segregation between the races. It resulted, as Plaatje shows, in the immediate expulsion of blacks, as "squatters", from their ancestral lands in the Orange Free State now declared "white". But Native Life succeeds in being much more than a work of propaganda. It is a vital social document which captures the spirit of an age and shows the effects of rural segregation on the everyday life of people.

Solomon Tshekeisho Plaatje was born in 1878 in the lands of the Tswana-speaking people, south of Mafeking. His origins were ordinary enough. What was remarkable was the aptitude he showed for education and learning after a few years schooling under the tuition of a remarkable liberal German Lutheran missionary, the Rev. Ludorf. At the age of sixteen Plaatje (using the Dutch nickname of his grandfather as a surname) joined the Post Office as a mail-carrier in Kimberley, the diamond city in the north of Cape Colony. He subsequently passed the highest clerical examination in the colony, beating every white candidate in both Dutch and typing.

From Kimberley the young Plaatje went on to Mafeking, where he was one of the key players in the great siege of 1899-1900. As magistrate's interpreter he was the vital link between the British civil authorities and the African majority beleaguered inside the town's military perimeter. Plaatje's diaries from this period, published long after his death, are a remarkable record both of the siege and of his early prose experimentation — mixing languages and idioms, and full of bright humour.

After the war Plaatje became a journalist, editor first of one Tswana language newspaper at Mafeking and then of another at Kimberley. Like other educated Africans he came out of the war optimistic that the British would enfranchise all educated and propertied males in the defeated Boer colonies (Transvaal and Orange Free State) without regard to race. But in this he, and the others, were soon sorely disappointed. The British gave a whites-only franchise to the defeated Boers and thus conceded power to a Boer or white Afrikaner parliamentary majority in the 1910 Union of South Africa which brought together the two Boer colonies with Cape Colony and Natal. Clinging to the old but diminished "colour blind" franchise of the Cape,

Plaatje remained one of the few Africans in South Africa with a parliamentary vote.

Plaatje's aggravation with the British government can be seen in an unpublished manuscript of 1908-09 titled "Sekgoma — the Black Dreyfus". In this booklet he castigated the British for denying legal rights (specifically habeas corpus) to their African subjects outside the Cape Colony.

Plaatje became politically active in the "native congress" movement which represented the interests of educated and propertied Africans all over South Africa. He was the first secretary-general of the "South African Native National Congress", founded in 1912 (which renamed itself as the African National Congress or ANC ten years later).

The first piece of major legislation presented to the whites-only parliament of South Africa was the Natives' Land Act, eventually passed in 1913, which was designed to entrench white power and property rights in the countryside — as well as to solve the "native problem" of African peasant farmers working for themselves and denying their labour power to white employers.

The main battle ground for the implementation of the new legislation was the Orange Free State. White farmers took the cue from the Land Act to begin expelling black peasants from their land as "squatters", while the police began to rigorously enforce the pass-laws which registered the employment of Africans and prescribed their residence and movement rights.

The Free State became the cockpit of resistance by the newly formed SANNC. Its womens' league demonstrated against pass law enforcement in Free State towns. Its national executive sent a delegation to England, icluding Plaatje, who set sail in mid-1914. The British crown retained ultimate rights of sovereignty over the parliament and government of South Africa, with an as yet unexercised power of veto over South African legislation in the area of "native affairs".

The delegation received short shrift from the government in London which was, after all, more than preoccupied with the coming of the Great War — in which it feared for the loyalty of the recently defeated Afrikaners and wished in no way to offend them. But, rather than return empty-handed like the rest of the SANNC delegation, Plaatje decided to stay in England to carry on the fight. He was determined to recuit, through writing and lecturing, the liberal and humanitarian establishment to his side — so that it in turn might pressure the British government.

Thus it was that Plaatje resumed work on a manuscript he had begun
on the ship to England. "Native Life in South Africa".
The book was published in 1916 by P. S. King in London.
It was dedicated to Harriette Colenso, doughty woman camnpaigner
who had inherited from her father, Bishop Colenso, the mantle of advocate
to the British establishment of the rights of the Zulu nation in South Africa.

While in England Plaatje pursued his interests in language and linguistics
by collaborating with Professor Daniel Jones of the University of London —
inventor of the International Phonetic Alphabet (IPA) and prototype for
Professor Higgins in Shaw's "Pygmalion" and thus the musical "My Fair Lady".
In the same year as Native Life was published, 1916, Plaatje published
two other shorter books which brought together the European languages
(English, Dutch and German) he loved with the Tswana language.
"Sechuana Proverbs" was a listing of Tswana proverbs with
their European equivalents. "A Sechuana Reader" was co-authored with Jones,
using the IPA for Tswana orthography.

Plaatje returned to South Africa but went once again to England
after the war's end, to lead a second SANNC delegation keen to make its mark
on the peace negotiations in 1919. This time Plaatje managed to get
as far as the prime minister, Lloyd George, "the Welsh wizard".
Lloyd George was duly impressed with Plaatje and undertook
to present his case to General Jan Smuts in the South African government,
a supposedly liberal fellow-traveller. But Smuts, whose notions of liberalism
were patronizingly segregationist, fobbed off Lloyd George
with an ingenuous reply.

Disillusioned with the flabby friendship of British liberals,
Plaatje was increasingly drawn to the pan-Africanism of W. E. B. Du Bois,
president of the NAACP in the United States. In 1921 Plaatje sailed
for the United States on a lecture tour that took him through
half the country. He paid his own way by publishing and selling
18,000 copies of a booklet titled "The Mote and the Beam: an Epic
on Sex-Relationship 'twixt Black and White in British South Africa"
at 25 cents each. In the following year, after Plaatje had left,
this new edition of "Native Life in South Africa" was published,
by the NAACP newspaper "The Crisis" edited by Du Bois.

Plaatje returned home to Kimberley to find the SANNC a spent force,
despite its name change to ANC, overtaken by more radical forces.
At a time when white power was pushing ahead with an ever more intense
segregationist programme, based on anti-black legislation,
Plaatje became a lone voice for old black liberalism. He turned from politics
and devoted the rest of his life to literature. His passion for Shakespeare
resulted in mellifluous Tswana translations of five plays
from "Comedy of Errors" to "Merchant of Venice" and "Julius Caesar".

His passion for the history of his people, and of his family in particular,
resulted in a historical novel, "Mhudi (An Epic of South African Native Life
a Hundred Years Ago)", dedicated to his daughter Olive who had died
in the influenza epidemic while Plaatje was overseas —
described in the dedication as "one of the many victims of a settled system".

"Mhudi" was published by the missionary press at Lovedale in 1930,
in a somewhat bowdlerized version. It has since been republished
in more pristine form and is today considered not just the first
but one of the very best novels published by a black South African writer
in English.

Plaatje lived an extraordinary life but died a largely disappointed man.
His feats of political journalism had been largely forgotten
and his creative talents had hardly yet been recognised
— except in the confined world of Tswana language readership.
But today Plaatje is regarded as a South African literary pioneer,
as a not insignificant political actor in his time,
and as a cogent commentator on his times. He was an explorer
in a fascinating world of cultural and linguistic interaction,
who was in retrospect truly a "renaissance man".

Related Reading:

Sol T. Plaatje (ed. John Comaroff with Brian Willan & Andrew Reed),
"Mafeking Diary: a Black Man's View of a White Man's War",
Athens, Ohio: Ohio University Press & Cambridge Meridor Press, 1990.
(1st edn. London: Macmillan, 1973, publ. as The Boer War Diary
of Sol T. Plaatje).

Sol. T. Plaatje (ed. Tim Couzens), "Mhudi", Cape Town: Francolin, 1996;
definitive edition.

Brian Willan, "Sol Plaatje: South African Nationalist, 1876-1932",
London: Heinemann, 1984.

Brian Willan (ed. & comp.), "Sol Plaatje: Selected Writings",
Athens, Ohio: Ohio University Press, 1996.

Neil Parsons is a Professor of History at the University of Botswana.
He is author of "King Khama, Emperor Joe, and the Great White Queen",
which details the journey of the Batswana delegation to England of 1895,
and other books relating to the history of the region.

To
Miss Harriette E. Colenso,

"Nkosazana Matotoba ka So-Bantu",
Daughter of the late Rt. Rev. J. W. Colenso
(In his life-time Bishop of Natal and "Father of the Zulus").

In recognition of her unswerving loyalty to
the policy of her late distinguished father
and unselfish interest in the welfare of
the South African Natives,

This Book is Dedicated.

Contents

(A) Who is the Author?
(B) Prologue
Chapter I A Retrospect
Chapter II The Grim Struggle between Right and Wrong, and the Latter Carries the Day
Chapter III The Natives' Land Act
Chapter IV One Night with the Fugitives
Chapter V Another Night with the Sufferers
Chapter VI Our Indebtedness to White Women
Chapter VII Persecution of Coloured Women in the Orange Free State
Chapter VIII At Thaba Ncho: A Secretarial Fiasco
Chapter IX The Fateful 13
Chapter X Dr. Abdurahman, President of the A.P.O. / Dr. A. Abdurahman, M.P.C.
Chapter XI The Natives' Land Act in Cape Colony
Chapter XII The Passing of Cape Ideals
Chapter XIII Mr. Tengo-Jabavu, the Pioneer Native Pressman
Chapter XIV The Native Congress and the Union Government
Chapter XV The Kimberley Congress / The Kimberley Conference
Chapter XVI The Appeal for Imperial Protection
Chapter XVII The London Press and the Natives' Land Act
Chapter XVIII The P.S.A. and Brotherhoods
Chapter XIX Armed Natives in the South African War
Chapter XX The South African Races and the European War
Chapter XXI Coloured People's Help Rejected / The Offer of Assistance by the South African Coloured Races Rejected
Chapter XXII The South African Boers and the European War
Chapter XXIII The Boer Rebellion
Chapter XXIV Piet Grobler
Epilogue
Report of the Lands Commission

(A) Who is the Author?

After wondering for some time how best to answer this question, we decided to reply to it by using one of several personal references in our possession. The next puzzle was: "Which one?" We carefully examined each, but could not strike a happy decision until some one who entered the room happened to make use of the familiar phrase: "The long and the short of it". That phrase solved the difficulty for us, and we at once made up our mind to use two of these references, namely, the shortest and the longest. The first one is from His Royal Highness the Duke of Connaught, and the second takes the form of a leading article in the 'Pretoria News'.

==

Central South African Railways,
High Commissioner's Train.

On February 1, 1906, Mr. Sol Plaatje acted as Interpreter when I visited the Barolong Native Stadt at Mafeking, and performed his duty to my entire satisfaction.

(Signed) Arthur.

Mafeking,
February 1, 1906.
==

== We commence to-day an experiment which will prove a success if only we can persuade the more rabid negrophobes to adopt a moderate and sensible attitude. We publish the first of a series of letters from a native correspondent of considerable education and ability, his name is Solomon Tshekisho Plaatje. Mr. Plaatje was born in the district of Boshof, his parents being Barolongs, coming originally from Thaba Ncho, and trekking eventually to Mafeking. He attended the Lutheran Mission School at the Pniel Mission Station, near Barkly West, as a boy, under the Rev. G. E. Westphal; and at thirteen years he passed the fourth standard, which was as far as the school could take him. For the next three years he acted as pupil-teacher, receiving private lessons from the Rev. and Mrs. Westphal. At the age of sixteen he joined the Cape Government service as letter-carrier in the Kimberley Post Office. There he studied languages in his spare time, and passed the Cape Civil Service examination in typewriting, Dutch and native languages, heading the list of successful candidates in each subject. Shortly before the war he was transferred to Mafeking as interpreter, and during the siege was appointed Dutch interpreter to the Court of Summary Jurisdiction, presided over by Lord Edward Cecil. The Magistrate's clerks having taken up arms, Mr. Plaatje became confidential clerk to Mr. C. G. H. Bell, who administered Native affairs during the siege. Mr. Plaatje drew up weekly reports on the Native situation, which were greatly valued by the military authorities, and in a letter written to a friend asserted with some sense of humour that "this arrangement was so satisfactory that Mr. Bell was created a C.M.G. at the end of the siege."

Had it not been for the colour bar, Mr. Plaatje, in all probability, would have been holding an important position in the Department of Native Affairs; as it was, he entered the ranks of journalism as Editor, in the first place, of `Koranta ea Becoana', a weekly paper in English and Sechuana, which was financed by the Chief Silas Molema and existed for seven years very successfully. At the present moment Mr. Plaatje is Editor of the `Tsala ea Batho' (The People's Friend) at Kimberley, which is owned by a native syndicate, having its headquarters in the Free State. Mr. Plaatje has acted as interpreter for many distinguished visitors to South Africa, and holds autograph letters from the Duke of Connaught, Mr. Chamberlain, and other notabilities. He visited Mr. Abraham Fischer quite lately and obtained from him a promise to introduce a Bill into Parliament ameliorating the position of the Natives of the Orange River Colony, who are debarred by law from receiving titles to landed property. Mr. Plaatje's articles on native affairs have been marked by the robust common sense and moderation so characteristic of Mr. Booker Washington. He realizes the great debt which the Natives owe to the men who brought civilization to South Africa. He is no agitator or firebrand, no stirrer-up of bad feeling between black and white. He accepts the position which the Natives occupy to-day in the body politic as the natural result of their lack of education and civilization. He is devoted to his own people, and notes with ever-increasing regret the lack of understanding and knowledge of those people, which is so palpable in the vast majority of the letters and leading articles written on the native question. As an educated Native with liberal ideas he rather resents the power and authority of the uneducated native chiefs who govern by virtue of their birth alone, and he writes and speaks for an entirely new school of native thought. The opinion of such a man ought to carry weight when native affairs are being discussed. We have fallen into the habit of discussing and legislating for the Native without ever stopping for one moment to consider what the Native himself thinks. No one but a fool will deny the importance of knowing what the Native thinks before we legislate for him. It is in the hope of enlightening an otherwise barren controversy that we shall publish from time to time Mr. Plaatje's letters, commending them always to the more thoughtful and practical of our readers. — `Pretoria News', September, 1910. ==

(The writer of this appreciation, the Editor of the Pretoria evening paper, was Reuter's war correspondent in the siege of Mafeking.)

(B) Prologue

We have often read books, written by well-known scholars, who disavow, on behalf of their works, any claim to literary perfection. How much more necessary, then, that a South African native workingman, who has never received any secondary training, should in attempting authorship disclaim, on behalf of his work, any title to literary merit. Mine is but a sincere narrative of a melancholy situation, in which, with all its shortcomings, I have endeavoured to describe the difficulties of the South African Natives under a very strange law, so as most readily to be understood by the sympathetic reader.

The information contained in the following chapters is the result of personal observations made by the author in certain districts of the Transvaal, Orange "Free" State and the Province of the Cape of Good Hope. In pursuance of this private inquiry, I reached Lady Brand early in September, 1913, when, my financial resources being exhausted, I decided to drop the inquiry and return home. But my friend, Mr. W. Z. Fenyang, of the farm Rietfontein, in the "Free" State, offered to convey me to the South of Moroka district, where I saw much of the trouble, and further, he paid my railway fare from Thaba Ncho back to Kimberley.

In the following November, it was felt that as Mr. Saul Msane, the organizer for the South African Native National Congress, was touring the eastern districts of the Transvaal, and Mr. Dube, the President, was touring the northern districts and Natal, and as the finances of the Congress did not permit an additional traveller, no information would be forthcoming in regard to the operation of the mischievous Act in the Cape Province. So Mr. J. M. Nyokong, of the farm Maseru, offered to bear part of the expenses if I would undertake a visit to the Cape. I must add that beyond spending six weeks on the tour to the Cape, the visit did not cost me much, for Mr. W. D. Soga, of King Williamstown, very generously supplemented Mr. Nyokong's offer and accompanied me on a part of the journey.

Besides the information received and the hospitality enjoyed from these and other friends, the author is indebted, for further information, to Mr. Attorney Msimang, of Johannesburg. Mr. Msimang toured some of the Districts, compiled a list of some of the sufferers from the Natives' Land Act, and learnt the circumstances of their eviction. His list, however, is not full, its compilation having been undertaken in May, 1914, when the main exodus of the evicted tenants to the cities and Protectorates had already taken place, and when eyewitnesses of the evils of the Act had already fled the country. But it is useful in showing that the persecution is still continuing, for, according to this list, a good many families were evicted a year after the Act was enforced, and many more were at that time under notice to quit. Mr. Msimang, modestly states in an explanatory note, that his pamphlet contains "comparatively few instances of actual cases of hardship under the Natives' Land Act, 1913, to vindicate the leaders of the South African Native National Congress from the gross imputation, by the Native Affairs Department, that they make general allegations of hardships without producing any specific cases that can bear examination." Mr. Msimang, who took a number of sworn statements from the sufferers, adds that "in Natal, for example, all of these instances have been reported to the Magistrates and the Chief Native Commissioner. Every time they are told to find themselves other places, or remain where they are under labour conditions. At Peters and Colworth, seventy-nine and a hundred families respectively are being ejected by the Government itself without providing land for them."

Some readers may perhaps think that I have taken the Colonial Parliament rather severely to task. But to any reader who holds with Bacon, that "the pencil hath laboured more in describing the afflictions of Job than the felicities of Solomon," I would say: "Do, if we dare make the request, and place yourself in our shoes." If, after a proper declaration of war, you found your kinsmen driven from pillar to post in the manner that the South African Natives have been harried and scurried by Act No. 27 of 1913, you would, though aware that it is part of the fortunes of war, find it difficult to suppress your hatred of the enemy. Similarly, if you see your countrymen and countrywomen driven from home, their homes broken up, with no hopes of redress, on the mandate of a Government to which they had loyally paid taxation without representation — driven from their homes, because they do not want to become servants; and when you know that half of these homeless ones have perforce submitted to the conditions and accepted service on terms that are unprofitable to themselves; if you remember that more would have submitted but for the fact that no master has any use for a servant with forty head of cattle, or a hundred or more sheep; and if you further bear in mind that many landowners are anxious to live at peace with, and to keep your people as tenants, but that they are debarred from doing so by your Government which threatens them with a fine of 100 Pounds or six months' imprisonment, you would, I think, likewise find it very difficult to maintain a level head or wield a temperate pen.

For instance, let us say, the London County Council decrees that no man shall rent a room, or hire a house, in the City of London unless he be a servant in the employ of the landlord, adding that there shall be a fine of one hundred pounds on any one who attempts to sell a house to a non-householder; imagine such a thing and its effects, then you have some approach to an accurate picture of the operation of the South African Natives' Land Act of 1913. In conclusion, let me ask the reader's support in our campaign for the repeal of such a law, and in making this request I pray that none of my readers may live to find themselves in a position so intolerable.

When the narrative of this book up to Chapter XVIII was completed, it was felt that an account of life in South Africa, without a reference to the war or the rebellion would be but a story half told, and so Chapters XIX-XXV were added. It will be observed that Chapters XX-XXIV, unlike the rest of the book, are not the result of the writer's own observations. The writer is indebted for much of the information in these five chapters to the Native Press and some Dutch newspapers which his devoted wife posted to him with every mail. These papers have been a source of useful information. Of the Dutch newspapers special thanks are due to `Het Westen' of Potchefstroom, which has since March 1915 changed its name to `Het Volksblad'. Most of the Dutch journals, especially in the northern Provinces, take up the views of English-speaking Dutch townsmen (solicitors and Bank clerks), and publish them as the opinion of the South African Dutch. `Het Westen' (now `Het Volksblad'), on the other hand, interprets the Dutch view, sound, bad or indifferent, exactly as we ourselves have heard it expressed by Dutchmen at their own farms.

Translations of the Tipperary Chorus into some of the languages which are spoken by the white and black inhabitants of South Africa have been used here and there as mottoes; and as this book is a plea in the main for help against the "South African war of extermination", it is hoped that admirers of Tommy Atkins will sympathize with the coloured sufferers, who also sing Tommy Atkins' war songs.

This appeal is not on behalf of the naked hordes of cannibals who are represented in fantastic pictures displayed in the shop-windows in Europe, most of them imaginary; but it is on behalf of five million loyal British subjects who shoulder "the black man's burden" every day, doing so without looking forward to any decoration or thanks. "The black man's burden" includes the faithful performance of all the unskilled and least paying labour in South Africa, the payment of direct taxation to the various Municipalities, at the rate of from 1s. to 5s. per mensum per capita (to develop and beautify the white quarters of the towns while the black quarters remain unattended) besides taxes to the Provincial and Central Government, varying from 12s. to 3 Pounds 12s. per annum, for the maintenance of Government Schools from which native children are excluded. In addition to these native duties and taxes, it is also part of "the black man's burden" to pay all duties levied from the favoured race. With the increasing difficulty of finding openings to earn the money for paying these multifarious taxes, the dumb pack-ox, being inarticulate in the Councils of State, has no means of making known to its "keeper" that the burden is straining its back to breaking point.

When Sir John French appealed to the British people for more shells during Easter week, the Governor-General of South Africa addressing a fashionable crowd at the City Hall, Johannesburg, most of whom had never seen the mouth of a mine, congratulated them on the fact that "under the strain of war and rebellion the gold industry had been maintained at full pitch," and he added that "every ounce of gold was worth many shells to the Allies." But His Excellency had not a word of encouragement for the 200,000 subterranean heroes who by day and by night, for a mere pittance, lay down their limbs and their lives to the familiar "fall of rock" and who, at deep levels ranging from 1,000 feet to 1,000 yards in the bowels of the earth, sacrifice their lungs to the rock dust which develops miners' phthisis and pneumonia — poor reward, but a sacrifice that enables the world's richest gold mines, in the Johannesburg area alone, to maintain the credit of the Empire with a weekly output of 750,000 Pounds worth of raw gold. Surely the appeal of chattels who render service of such great value deserves the attention of the British people.

Finally, I would say as Professor Du Bois says in his book `The Souls of Black Folk', on the relations between the sons of master and man, "I have not glossed over matters for policy's sake, for I fear we have already gone too far in that sort of thing. On the other hand I have sincerely sought to let no unfair exaggerations creep in. I do not doubt that in some communities conditions are better than those I have indicated; while I am no less certain that in other communities they are far worse."

Chapter I A Retrospect

I am Black, but comely, O ye daughters of Jerusalem, as the tents of Kedar,
as the curtains of Solomon.
Look not upon me because I am black, because the sun hath looked upon me:
my mother's children were angry with me; they made me
the keeper of the vineyards; but mine own vineyard have I not kept.
The Song of Songs.

Awaking on Friday morning, June 20, 1913, the South African Native found himself, not actually a slave, but a pariah in the land of his birth.

The 4,500,000 black South Africans are domiciled as follows: One and three-quarter millions in Locations and Reserves, over half a million within municipalities or in urban areas, and nearly a million as squatters on farms owned by Europeans. The remainder are employed either on the public roads or railway lines, or as servants by European farmers, qualifying, that is, by hard work and saving to start farming on their own account.

A squatter in South Africa is a native who owns some livestock and, having no land of his own, hires a farm or grazing and ploughing rights from a landowner, to raise grain for his own use and feed his stock. Hence, these squatters are hit very hard by an Act which passed both Houses of Parliament during the session of 1913, received the signature of the Governor-General on June 16, was gazetted on June 19, and forthwith came into operation. It may be here mentioned that on that day Lord Gladstone signed no fewer than sixteen new Acts of Parliament — some of them being rather voluminous — while three days earlier, His Excellency signed another batch of eight, of which the bulk was beyond the capability of any mortal to read and digest in four days.

But the great revolutionary change thus wrought by a single stroke of the pen, in the condition of the Native, was not realized by him until about the end of June. As a rule many farm tenancies expire at the end of the half-year, so that in June, 1913, not knowing that it was impracticable to make fresh contracts, some Natives unwittingly went to search for new places of abode, which some farmers, ignorant of the law, quite as unwittingly accorded them. It was only when they went to register the new tenancies that the law officers of the Crown laid bare the cruel fact that to provide a landless Native with accommodation was forbidden under a penalty of 100 Pounds, or six months' imprisonment. Then only was the situation realized.

Other Natives who had taken up fresh places on European farms under verbal contracts, which needed no registration, actually founded new homes in spite of the law, neither the white farmer nor the native tenant being aware of the serious penalties they were exposed to by their verbal contracts.

In justice to the Government, it must be stated that no police officers scoured the country in search of lawbreakers, to prosecute them under this law. Had this been done, many 100 Pound cheques would have passed into the Government coffers during that black July, the first month after Lord Gladstone affixed his signature to the Natives' Land Act, No. 27 of 1913.

The complication of this cruel law is made manifest by the fact that it was found necessary for a high officer of the Government to tour the Provinces soon after the Act came into force, with the object of "teaching" Magistrates how to administer it. A Congress of Magistrates — a most unusual thing — was also called in Pretoria to find a way for carrying out the King's writ in the face of the difficulties arising from this tangle of the Act. We may add that nearly all white lawyers in South Africa, to whom we spoke about this measure, had either not seen the Act at all, or had not read it carefully, so that in both cases they could not tell exactly for whose benefit it had been passed. The study of this law required a much longer time than the lawyers, unless specially briefed, could devote to it, so that they hardly knew what all the trouble was about. It was the Native in the four Provinces who knew all about it, for he had not read it in books but had himself been through its mill, which like an automatic machine ground him relentlessly since the end of the month of June. Not the least but one of the cruellest and most ironical phases — and nearly every clause of this Act teems with irony — is the Schedule or appendix giving the so-called Scheduled Native Areas; and what are these "Scheduled Native Areas"?

They are the Native Locations which were reserved for the exclusive use of certain native clans. They are inalienable and cannot be bought or sold, yet the Act says that in these "Scheduled Native Areas" Natives only may buy land. The areas being inalienable, not even members of the clans, for whose benefit the locations are held in trust, can buy land therein. The areas could only be sold if the whole clan rebelled; in that case the location would be confiscated. But as long as the clans of the location remain loyal to the Government, nobody can buy any land within these areas. Under the respective charters of these areas, not even a member of the clan can get a separate title as owner in an area — let alone a native outsider who had grown up among white people and done all his farming on white man's land.

If we exclude the arid tracts of Bechuanaland, these Locations appear to have been granted on such a small scale that each of them got so overcrowded that much of the population had to go out and settle on the farms of white farmers through lack of space in the Locations. Yet a majority of the legislators, although well aware of all these limitations, and without remedying any of them, legislate, shall we say, "with its tongue in its cheek" that only Natives may buy land in Native Locations.

Again, the Locations form but one-eighteenth of the total area of the Union. Theoretically, then, the 4,500,000 Natives may "buy" land in only one-eighteenth part of the Union, leaving the remaining seventeen parts for the one million whites. It is moreover true that, numerically, the Act was passed by the consent of a majority of both Houses of Parliament, but it is equally true that it was steam-rolled into the statute book against the bitterest opposition of the best brains of both Houses. A most curious aspect of this singular law is that even the Minister, since deceased, who introduced it, subsequently declared himself against it, adding that he only forced it through in order to stave off something worse. Indeed, it is correct to say that Mr. Sauer, who introduced the Bill, spoke against it repeatedly in the House; he deleted the milder provisions, inserted more drastic amendments, spoke repeatedly against his own amendments, then in conclusion he would combat his own arguments by calling the ministerial steam-roller to support the Government and vote for the drastic amendments. The only explanation of the puzzle constituted as such by these "hot-and-cold" methods is that Mr. Sauer was legislating for an electorate, at the expense of another section of the population which was without direct representation in Parliament. None of the non-European races in the Provinces of Natal, Transvaal and the "Free" State can exercise the franchise. They have no say in the selection of members for the Union Parliament. That right is only limited to white men, so that a large number of the members of Parliament who voted for this measure have no responsibility towards the black races.

Before reproducing this tyrannical enactment it would perhaps be well to recapitulate briefly the influences that led up to it. When the Union of the South African Colonies became an accomplished fact, a dread was expressed by ex-Republicans that the liberal native policy of the Cape would supersede the repressive policy of the old Republics, and they lost no time in taking definite steps to force down the throats of the Union Legislature, as it were, laws which the Dutch Presidents of pre-war days, with the British suzerainty over their heads, did not dare enforce against the Native people then under them. With the formation of the Union, the Imperial Government, for reasons which have never been satisfactorily explained, unreservedly handed over the Natives to the colonists, and these colonists, as a rule, are dominated by the Dutch Republican spirit. Thus the suzerainty of Great Britain, which under the reign of Her late Majesty Victoria, of blessed memory, was the Natives' only bulwark, has now apparently been withdrawn or relaxed, and the Republicans, like a lot of bloodhounds long held in the leash, use the free hand given by the Imperial Government not only to guard against a possible supersession of Cape ideals of toleration, but to effectively extend throughout the Union the drastic native policy pursued by the Province which is misnamed "Free" State, and enforce it with the utmost rigour.

During the first year of the Union, it would seem that General Botha made an honest attempt to live up to his London promises, that are mentioned by Mr. Merriman in his speech (reproduced elsewhere) on the second reading of the Bill in Parliament. It would seem that General Botha endeavoured to allay British apprehensions and concern for the welfare of the Native population. In pursuance of this policy General Botha won the approbation of all Natives by appointing Hon. H. Burton, a Cape Minister, to the portfolio of Native Affairs. That the appointment was a happy one, from the native point of view, became manifest when Mr. Burton signalized the ushering in of Union, by releasing Chief Dinizulu-ka-Cetywayo, who at that time was undergoing a sentence of imprisonment imposed by the Natal Supreme Court, and by the restoration to Dinizulu of his pension of 500 Pounds a year. Also, in deference to the wishes of the Native Congress, Mr. Burton abrogated two particularly obnoxious Natal measures, one legalizing the "Sibalo" system of forced labour, the other prohibiting public meetings by Natives without the consent of the Government. These abrogations placed the Natives of Natal in almost the same position as the Cape Natives though without giving them the franchise. So, too, when a drastic Squatters' Bill was gazetted early in 1912, and the recently formed Native National Congress sent a deputation to interview Mr. Burton in Capetown; after hearing the deputation, he graciously consented to withdraw the proposed measure, pending the allotment of new Locations in which Natives evicted by such a measure could find an asylum. In further deference to the representations of the Native Congress, in which they were supported by Senators the Hon. W. P. Schreiner, Colonel Stanford, and Mr. Krogh, the Union Government gazetted another Bill in January, 1911, to amend an anomaly which, at that time, was peculiar to the "Free" State: an anomaly under which a Native can neither purchase nor lease land, and native landowners in the "Free" State could only sell their land to the white people.

The gazetted Bill proposed to legalize only in one district of the Orange "Free" State the sale of landed property by a Native to another Native as well as to a white man, but it did not propose to enable Natives to buy land from white men. The object of the Bill was to remove a hardship, mentioned elsewhere in this sketch, by which a "Free" State Native was by law debarred from inheriting landed property left to him under his uncle's will. But against such small attempts at reform, proposed or carried out by the Union Government in the interest of the Natives, granted in small instalments of a teaspoonful at a time — reforms dictated solely by feelings of justice and equity — ex-Republicans were furious.

From platform, Press, and pulpit it was suggested that General Botha's administration was too pro-English and needed overhauling. The Dutch peasants along the countryside were inflamed by hearing that their gallant leader desired to Anglicize the country. Nothing was more repellent to the ideas of the backveld Dutch, and so at small meetings in the country districts resolutions were passed stating that the Botha administration had outlived its usefulness. These resolutions reaching the Press from day to day had the effect of stirring up the Dutch voters against the Ministry, and particularly against the head. At this time General Botha's sound policy began to weaken. He transferred Hon. H. Burton, first Minister of Natives, to the portfolio of Railways and Harbours, and appointed General Hertzog, of all people in the world, to the portfolio of Native Affairs.

The good-humoured indulgence of some Dutch and English farmers towards their native squatters, and the affectionate loyalty of some of these native squatters in return, will cause a keen observer, arriving at a South African farm, to be lost in admiration for this mutual good feeling. He will wonder as to the meaning of the fabled bugbear anent the alleged struggle between white and black, which in reality appears to exist only in the fertile brain of the politician. Thus let the new arrival go to one of the farms in the Bethlehem or Harrismith Districts for example, and see how willingly the Native toils in the fields; see him gathering in his crops and handing over the white farmer's share of the crop to the owner of the land; watch the farmer receiving his tribute from the native tenants, and see him deliver the first prize to the native tenant who raised the largest crop during that season; let him also see both the Natives and the landowning white farmers following to perfection the give-and-take policy of "live and let live", and he will conclude that it would be gross sacrilege to attempt to disturb such harmonious relations between these people of different races and colours. But with a ruthless hand the Natives' Land Act has succeeded in remorselessly destroying those happy relations.

First of all, General Hertzog, the new Minister of Native Affairs, travelled up and down the country lecturing farmers on their folly in letting ground to the Natives; the racial extremists of his party hailed him as the right man for the post, for, as his conduct showed them, he would soon "fix up" the Natives. At one or two places he was actually welcomed as the future Prime Minister of the Union. On the other hand, General Botha, who at that time seemed to have become visibly timid, endeavoured to ingratiate himself with his discontented supporters by joining his lieutenant in travelling to and fro, denouncing the Dutch farmers for not expelling the Natives from their farms and replacing them with poor whites. This became a regular Ministerial campaign against the Natives, so that it seemed clear that if any Native could still find a place in the land, it was not due to the action of the Government. In his campaign the Premier said other unhappy things which were diametrically opposed to his London speeches of two years before; and while the Dutch colonists railed at him for trying to Anglicize the country, English speakers and writers justly accused him of speaking with two voices; cartoonists, too, caricatured him as having two heads — one, they said, for London, and the second one for South Africa.

The uncertain tenure by which Englishmen in the public service held their posts became the subject of debates in the Union Parliament, and the employment of Government servants of colour was decidedly precarious. They were swept out of the Railway and Postal Service with a strong racial broom, in order to make room for poor whites, mainly of Dutch descent. Concession after concession was wrung from the Government by fanatical Dutch postulants for office, for Government doles and other favours, who, like the daughters of the horse-leech in the Proverbs of Solomon, continually cried, "Give, give." By these events we had clearly turned the corner and were pacing backwards to pre-Union days, going back, back, and still further backward, to the conditions which prevailed in the old Republics, and (if a check is not applied) we shall steadily drift back to the days of the old Dutch East Indian administration.

The Bill which proposed to ameliorate the "Free" State cruelty, to which reference has been made above, was dropped like a hot potato. Ministers made some wild and undignified speeches, of which the following spicy extract, from a speech by the Rt. Hon. Abraham Fischer to his constituents at Bethlehem, is a typical sample —

"What is it you want?" he asked. "We have passed all the coolie* laws and we have passed all the Kafir laws. The `Free' State has been safeguarded and all her colour laws have been adopted by Parliament. What more can the Government do for you?" And so the Union ship in this reactionary sea sailed on and on and on, until she struck an iceberg — the sudden dismissal of General Hertzog.

— * A contemptuous South African term for British Indians. —

To the bitter sorrow of his admirers, General Hertzog, who is the fearless exponent of Dutch ideals, was relieved of his portfolios of Justice and Native Affairs — it was whispered as a result of a suggestion from London; and then the Dutch extremists, in consequence of their favourite's dismissal, gave vent to their anger in the most disagreeable manner. One could infer from their platform speeches that, from their point of view, scarcely any one else had any rights in South Africa, and least of all the man with a black skin.

In the face of this, the Government's timidity was almost unendurable. They played up to the desires of the racial extremists, with the result that a deadlock overtook the administration. Violent laws like the Immigration Law (against British Indians and alien Asiatics) and the Natives' Land were indecently hurried through Parliament to allay the susceptibilities of "Free" State Republicans. No Minister found time to undertake such useful legislation as the Coloured People's Occupation Bill, the Native Disputes Bill, the Marriage Bill, the University Bill, *etc.*, *etc.* An apology was demanded from the High Commissioner in London for delivering himself of sentiments which were felt to be too British for the palates of his Dutch employers in South Africa, and the Prime Minister had almost to apologize for having at times so far forgotten himself as to act more like a Crown Minister than a simple Africander. "Free" State demands became so persistent that Ministers seemed to have forgotten the assurances they gave His Majesty's Government in London regarding the safety of His Majesty's coloured subjects within the Union. They trampled under foot their own election pledges, made during the first Union General Election, guaranteeing justice and fair treatment to the law-abiding Natives.

The campaign, to compass the elimination of the blacks from the farms, was not at all popular with landowners, who made huge profits out of the renting of their farms to Natives. Platform speakers and newspaper writers coined an opprobrious phrase which designated this letting of farms to Natives as "Kafir-farming", and attempted to prove that it was almost as immoral as "baby-farming". But landowners pocketed the annual rents, and showed no inclination to substitute the less industrious "poor whites" for the more industrious Natives. Old Baas M——, a typical Dutch landowner of the "Free" State, having collected his share of the crop of 1912, addressing a few words of encouragement to his native tenants, on the subject of expelling the blacks from the farms, said in the Taal: "How dare any number of men, wearing tall hats and frock coats, living in Capetown hotels at the expense of other men, order me to evict my Natives? This is my ground; it cost my money, not Parliament's, and I will see them banged (barst) before I do it."

It then became evident that the authority of Parliament would have to be sought to compel the obstinate landowners to get rid of their Natives. And the compliance of Parliament with this demand was the greatest Ministerial surrender to the Republican malcontents, resulting in the introduction and passage of the Natives' Land Act of 1913, inasmuch as the Act decreed, in the name of His Majesty the King, that pending the adoption of a report to be made by a commission, somewhere in the dim and unknown future, it shall be unlawful for Natives to buy or lease land, except in scheduled native areas. And under severe pains and penalties they were to be deprived of the bare human rights of living on the land, except as servants in the employ of the whites — rights which were never seriously challenged under the Republican regime, no matter how politicians raved against the Natives.

Chapter II The Grim Struggle between Right and Wrong, and the Latter Carries the Day

Woe unto them that decree unrighteous decrees, and that write grievousness
which they have prescribed;
To turn aside the needy from judgment, and to take away the fruit
from the poor of my people, that widows may be their prey,
and that they may rob the fatherless.
Isaiah.

On February 18, 1913, General L. Lemmer, member for Marico, Transvaal, asked the Minister of Lands: — (a) How many farms or portions of farms in the Transvaal Province have during the last three years been registered in the names of Natives; (b) what is the extent of the land so registered; and (c) how much was paid for it?

The Minister of Lands replied: (a) 78 farms; (b) 144,416 morgen; and (c) 94,907 Pounds.

Some very disturbing elements suggest themselves in this question and in its prompt answer. A question of the kind should have taken some time to reach Pretoria from the seat of Parliament; more time to search for and compile the necessary information, and further time to get the answer to the Table of the House of Assembly in Capetown. For instance, on March 11 Mr. T. L. Schreiner called for an explanation in connexion with the same return. He had to ask again on April 1, the answer in each instance being that the required "information had been telegraphed for and would be laid on the table when it is available" (vide Union Hansard, pp. 777 and 1,175). It was only on May 13 — two months and two days after — that an answer to Mr. Schreiner's question of March 11 could be furnished.

Again, on May 20 Mr. Schreiner called for a similar return, embracing the four Provinces of the Union.* If it were so easy for General Lemmer to get a reply in regard to the Transvaal, where most of the registration took place, it should have been relatively more easy to add the information from the Cape and Natal, since no registration could have taken place in the Orange "Free" State, where Natives cannot buy land. But strange to say, all that Mr. Schreiner could get out of the Minister was a promise to furnish a reply when it is available, and it does not appear to be on record that it was ever furnished during that session. Therefore, a Native cannot be blamed for suspecting that when General Lemmer asked his question, the return was "cut and dried" and available to be laid on the table as soon as it was called for.

— * It does not appear to have occurred to any one to call for a return
  showing transfers of land from blacks to whites.
—

Another significant point is that the questioner did not want to know the extent of land bought by Natives, but of the land "registered in their names" during the period;

and Mr. Schreiner was able to show later in the session by an analysis of the return that it mainly comprised land awarded to Native tribes by the Republican Government, some of it when they conquered the country. They include farms bought or awarded to Natives as long ago as the early 60's and 70's, but the owners were not able to obtain titles as the late Republican Government did not allow Natives to register land in their own names. They had been held in trust for them by European friends or missionaries, and it was only during the last three years that the owners claimed direct titles, which right was restored to them since the British occupation.

But the Lemmer Return did its fell work. It scared every white man in the country. They got alarmed to hear that Natives had during the past three (!) years "bought" land to the extent of 50,000 morgen per annum.

Thanks to Mr. Schreiner's questions, however, the misleading features of the statistical scarecrow were revealed — but, unfortunately too late.

Origin of the Trouble

On February 28, 1913, Mr. J. G. Keyter (a "Free" State member) moved: That the Government be requested to submit to the House *during the present session* a general Pass and Squatters Bill to prohibit coloured people (1) from *wandering about without* A *proper pass*; (2) from *squatting on farms*; and (3) from *sowing on the share system*.

Mr. T. P. Brain,* another "Free" Stater, seconded the motion.

— * This gentleman died during 1913. —

Mr. P. G. W. Grobler,* a Transvaaler, moved (as an amendment) to add at the end of the motion: "and further *to take effective measures to restrict the purchase and lease of land by natives*."

— * Mr. Grobler forfeited his seat when he was convicted of complicity
  in the recent rebellion.
—

Mr. Schreiner strongly protested against both the motion and the amendment.

The Minister for Native Affairs* spoke somewhat against Mr. Keyter's motion but promised to comply with Mr. Grobler's amendment, which promise he redeemed by introducing a Natives' Land Bill.

— * Hon. J. W. Sauer, Minister of Native Affairs, died a month after the Bill
  became law.
—

Before the Bill was introduced, the Minister made the unprecedented announcement that the Governor-General had given his assurance that the Royal Assent would not be withheld from the Natives' Land Bill. Section 65 of the South African Constitution provides that the King may disallow an Act of Parliament within twelve months after the Governor-General signed it. And the abrogation of the Constitution, as far as this Bill is concerned, literally gave licence to the political libertines of South Africa; as, being thus freed from all legislative restraint, they wasted no further time listening to such trifles as reason and argument.

The following are extracts from the debates on the Natives' Land Bill as reported in the Union Hansard of 1913.

== The adjourned debate on the motion for the second reading of the Natives Land Bill was resumed by

Mr. J. X. *Merriman* (Victoria West). It was with very great reluctance (the right hon. gentleman said) that he rose to speak on this measure. It would have been more convenient to have given a silent vote, but he felt, and he was afraid, that after many years of devoted attention to this question of the native policy of South Africa, he would not be doing his duty if he did not give this House — for what it was worth — the result of his experience through these years.

He should like to emphasize a brighter side of the question, and that was to point out that the Natives, if they were well managed, were an invaluable asset to the people of this country. (Hear, hear.) Let them take our trade figures and compare them with the trade figures of the other large British Dominions. Our figures were surprising when measured by the white population, but if they took the richest Dominion that there was under the British Crown outside South Africa, and took the trade value of those figures per head of the white population, and multiply those figures by our European population, then they might very well apply any balance they had to our native population, and then they would see, strangely enough, that upon that basis it worked out that the actual trade of three Natives was worth about that of one white man. That, of course, was a very imperfect way of looking at the value of these people, because the trade value of some of these Natives was far greater than the trade value of some of our white people. He had merely indicated these trade figures to show what an enormous asset we had in the Natives in that respect. Let them think what the industry of the Natives had done for us. Who had built our railways, who had dug our mines, and developed this country as far as it was developed? Who had been the actual manual worker who had done that? The Native: the coloured races of this country. We must never forget that we owed them a debt in that respect — a debt not often acknowledged by what we did for them. Proceeding, he said that they ought to think what they owed to the docility of the Natives, and the wonderfully easy way in which they had been governed when treated properly. He also paid a tribute to the honesty of the Natives.

What must strike any one was the fact that though this Bill was really, to a certain extent, a beginning, or was thought to be in certain quarters, of a revolution in their dealing with the native races, it was not even mentioned in the speech of the Governor-General. It fell upon them like a bolt from the blue. He remembered the afternoon. They had heard a very impassioned and very heated speech from the hon. member for Ficksburg on the enormous danger of squatting in the Free State, and that was the occasion for introducing a general statement of the policy of the Government towards the Natives and the introduction of this Bill. He did not think that that was the way they liked to see a thing of this magnitude approached. They often heard demands for what was called a general declaration of policy with regard to native affairs — a policy which should be applied to the highest civilized Native, the owner of a farm, and the naked barbarian. They could not do it. People who demanded a general declaration of that kind had not had the experience which some of them had had. The hon. member who spoke before him said that he was in favour of the underlying principle of the Bill. What was the underlying principle? The underlying principle was what one read into the Bill. One hon. member read into it that it was the separation of the two races. That might have been done when the two races first came in contact at the Fish River, but it could not be done now. Since then they had been developing the country with the labour of these people. They had been advancing by our aid. They had mixed themselves up with these people in an inextricable fashion and then some said "Haul your native policy out of the drawer and begin with a policy of separation." He was sure that the hon. member who had brought in the Bill had no idea of that sort in his mind. Another person had the idea that they were going to set up a sort of pale — a sort of kraal in which they were going to drive these people. Then another gentleman sneered at the policy hitherto adopted, and he said that one side said that the policy towards the Natives should be firm and just, while the other side said that it should be just and firm.

It seemed to him that they had not got sufficient information. Beyond the bald statistics which were given by the Minister in the course of his interesting and moderate speech, they had nothing. They were going into a thing that would stir South Africa from end to end, and which affected hundreds of thousands of both races. They had no information as to what were the ideas of the Natives. It was unfortunate that, owing to this lack of information, wrong ideas had got about with regard to this Bill. It was difficult to find out what the Native thought about these things; he doubted whether anybody could say that he had got at the mind of the Native. The only way, and he must say that he did not take it as a real indication, was what they wrote in their newspapers. He was alarmed, but not surprised, at some of the articles in their newspapers, because they took their views from the heated speeches and writings in party newspapers all over the country, and they were very much alarmed. He thought that before a Bill of this sort was passed, there should be some attempt made to get their views. As far as one section was concerned, the Bill was going to set up a sort of pale — that there was going to be a sort of kraal in which all the Natives were to be driven, and they were to be left to develop on their own lines. To allow them to go on their own lines was merely to drive them back into barbarism; their own lines meant barbarous lines; their own lines were cruel lines. All along they had been bringing them away from their own lines. It reminded him of what an English writer said about a similar policy in Ireland, because when the English went to Ireland they regarded the Native Irish in the way some extreme people here regarded the Natives of South Africa. They thought they would root them out. They treated them as dogs, and thought that they were dogs. They set up a pale. They set the Irish within that pale, to develop upon their own lines, but there were always Englishmen living in that pale, just as in the same way they found Europeans living among Natives. Sir George Davis in describing this policy wrote that it was the intention of the Government to set up a separation between English and Irish, intending in time that the English should root out the Irish. If they changed the Irish for Natives they would see how the illustration would apply. A policy more foredoomed to failure in South Africa could not be initiated. It was a policy that would keep South Africa back, perhaps for ever. (Hear, hear.) What would be the effect of driving these civilized Natives back into reserves? At the present time, every civilized man — if they treated him properly — every civilized man was becoming an owner of land outside native reserve, and therefore he was an asset of strength to the country. He was a loyalist. He was not going to risk losing his property. He was on the side of the European. If they drove these people back into reserve they became our bitterest enemies. Therefore, he viewed anything that tended that way with the gravest suspicion. Again, in this Bill there was not sufficient distinction between those Natives who tried to educate themselves and the ordinary raw barbarian. They were all classed under the word "Native".

He came now to what was the main object of the Bill, and that was: to do away with the squatting evil. Why was there a squatting evil? Was it the fault of the Native? (An hon. member: No.) Was it the fault of the law? (No.) They had got the most stringent laws concerning Natives of all the laws in the whole country, in the Province of which his hon. friend (Mr. Keyter) was a member. He did not think anything was more surprising than when they came to look at the increases in the native population in the Orange Free State. They had a huge native population in the Cape, and the increase during the census periods from 1904 to 1911 — he wanted hon. members to pay some attention to this, because it showed the value of legislation — the increase in the Cape Province during that period was 8.33 per cent. In Natal, which had a huge — in fact, an overwhelming — native population, curiously enough, the increase was the same, even to the actual decimal figure, *viz.*, 8.33 per cent.: but some allowance must be made, because a large number of Natives were out at work in the mines. Now, in the Transvaal — and in taking the Transvaal figures these did not apply as regarded squatting, because the increase was mainly due to the number of Natives employed in the mines. In the Transvaal the Natives increased by 30.1 per cent. Now, when they came to his friend's little State, where the most stringent laws were made to keep out the Natives, how much did they suppose the Natives increased in the Free State? By no less than 44 per cent. (Opposition cheers.) Was that the fault of the Natives? No, it was because — having the most stringent laws — the people found it best to evade those laws. (Hear, hear.) He hoped his hon. friend would be a little tolerant. Do let him pick the mote out of his own eye before he tried to pick the beam out of other people's. (Hear, hear.) In the Free State these laws were very severe; for instance, punishments — amazing punishments — were given, and yet the result was the increase in five years by 44 per cent. of their native population. This was something that they should take a warning by. They were going to do away with the squatter in appearance, but he would still survive as a labour tenant. They might do away with the labour tenant, and he would still be surviving as a labour servant. How was the Government to distinguish between these? They had in the Cape a law which stated how many labour tenants a man should have upon his farm.

What they wanted in this country was administration and not more legislation, and if they were to put the laws which they had into force in the Free State at the present time he had no doubt that there would be a rebellion. (Hear, hear.) They would have platforms swarming with people who would say that they could not grow one bag of mealies without the Natives. But they had the laws to do it. Now they went and tried in this Bill to make a uniform law. Turning towards the Minister, Mr. Merriman said: "My poor friend! that after all the years we had laboured together he of all people should be the author of a uniform law on native matters! (Laughter.) I say this more in sorrow than in anger — (laughter) — because the conditions were totally different in the four Provinces."

In the Free State, proceeded Mr. Merriman, the people had most excellent laws from their point of view for keeping out the Natives — stringent, Draconian, and violent laws, but they were not carried out, and the Natives had flooded the country. All they wanted to do was to turn the Native from a tenant to a labour tenant, and then salvation would be at hand. He could not see very much difference between the two, except that one was a contented advancing man and the other a discontented man approaching very closely to the Russian serf — he was a soul. Shortly we should hear of a farm being up for sale with so many souls.

In the Transvaal the problem had been complicated by the decisions of the Court and the curious way in which some ground had been given out in the Zoutpansberg district, where, he was told, farms had been given out on which the Natives had been living for years, and these farms — with the Natives on them — had come into the possession of companies and individuals, and now it was proposed to turn the Natives off. That would not be an agreeable thing, but he would not offer an opinion now as to the justice of it.

He would like to revert to the state of things which had grown up under the Draconian laws of the Free State. According to a very interesting Blue-book containing reports of magistrates, one magistrate had reported that "the pernicious system of squatting was detrimental to the working farmer, the Native reaping the whole of the benefit." The man who worked generally reaped the whole benefit in the long run. In the Harrismith district there were some 40,000 Natives against some 8,000 Europeans. How did they get there? Having been a Free State burgher he knew that the Natives had not forced their way in. These Natives ploughed on the half-shares, and he would like to know whether they were labour tenants or squatters. If they were squatters it would require very little dexterous management to convert them into labour tenants. The Magistrate of Hoopstad, went on Mr. Merriman, had referred to the pernicious system of native squatters. But why did not the Free State magistrates do something and put the law in force? That was the principal reason why the House was forced to pass that Bill without information, and without giving any opportunity to people who had the deepest interest in this matter to have their views heard, or to let them know what the House was going to do because the magistrates in the Free State would not enforce the law. He did think that was rather hard. In conclusion Mr. Merriman said: I dare say I may have said a great many things which may be distasteful to my hon. friends, but I do claim their attention because at a time when they were not in such a dominant position as they are now, I pleaded for right and justice for them. Therefore, they should not take it amiss from me, because now they are in a dominant position, I plead also for justice, toleration, moderation, and delay in this matter.

Mr. H. Mentz (Zoutpansberg) said the right hon. gentleman had earned their gratitude for the high tone in which he had carried the debate. The speech which he had delivered was a most instructive one, and although the speaker was not in entire agreement with him on all points, he was in agreement on the point that the matter was one to be handled with prudence, but it was to be regretted that under the Bill a Commission was to be appointed. The Minister should not listen to the request for a postponement of the question, by referring it to a Select Committee. If they were to refer the Bill to a Select Committee, it would never be passed this year.

Mr. G. L. Steytler (Rouxville) expressed his thanks to the Government for bringing forward the Bill. He said he felt that it was not a complete solution of the whole question, but it was certainly a step in the right direction.

Mr. A. Fawcus (Umlazi) said that as the representative of 70,000 Natives in Natal, not one of whom so far as he knew had a vote, he should like, on their behalf, to thank the right hon. member for Victoria West for the manner in which he had handled this question. In the course of his speech the right hon. gentleman asked, what did the Natives think about this Bill before the House? His (Mr. Fawcus') opinion was that the Natives did not think anything at all about it. He should not think there was one Native in a thousand in South Africa who was aware that this matter, so vitally affecting their future, was at present at issue. The hon. member for Middelburg had referred to the Natives as "schepsels".* He believed the day was rapidly passing away when we should refer to Natives as "schepsels". They were an easy-going folk, and they thought little about title deeds and land laws. So great was the Native's attachment to the land on which he lived, in many instances, that they could not rackrent him off it. These were the people that the Bill wished to dispossess and drive off the land. The figures placed before them showed that *the land held by Europeans per head was fifty times the amount held per head by the natives.* Surely there was no need at the present time for legislation which would prevent Natives getting a little more land than they now had. He did not think it could be put down to the fault of the Native if he was willing to buy and live on land rather than pay rent. The figures given in this connexion were very instructive. *Eight Acres per head were held by the natives in the Cape, six Acres in Natal, about 1 1/2 Acres* in the Transvaal, and about one-third of an acre in the Free State. He thought this Bill was perhaps coming on a little before there was any necessity for it.

— * Creatures. —

Mr. C. G. FICHARDT (Ladybrand) said he felt very much that the Bill that was before the House did not carry out all that should be carried out, and that was equality of justice. *If they were to deal fairly with the natives of this country, then according to population they should give them four-fifths of the country, or at least A half.* How were they going to do that? As he said in the earlier part of his remarks, he was prepared to accept the Bill as something to go on with, but he hoped that in the future it would not constitute a stumbling-block. He would much rather have seen that the matter had been gone into more fully, and that some scheme had been laid before them so that they might have more readily been able to judge how the Bill would work. It was because of all these difficulties that he felt that they could only accept the Bill if it laid down that there was no intention of taking the country from the white people and handing it over to the blacks.

Mr. J. G. Keyter (Ficksburg) said he wished to openly denounce, and most emphatically so, that the people or the Government of the Orange Free State had treated the coloured people unreasonably or unjustly, or in any way oppressively. On the contrary, the O.F.S. had always treated the coloured people with the greatest consideration and the utmost justice. The O.F.S. had made what Mr. Merriman called stringent laws. He (Mr. Keyter) called them just laws. They *told the coloured people plainly that the* O.F.S. *Was A white man's country, and that they intended to keep it so.* (Hear, hear.) *They told the coloured people that they were not to be allowed to buy or hire land*, and that they were not going to tolerate an equality of whites and blacks; and he said that they were not going to tolerate that in the future, and if an attempt were made to force that on them, they would resist it at any cost to the last,* for if they did tolerate it, they would very soon find that they would be a bastard nation. His experience was that the Native should be treated firmly, kept in his place and treated honestly. They should not give him a gun one day and fight him for it the next day. They should tell him, as the Free State told him, that *it was A white man's country, that he was not going to be allowed to buy land there or to hire land there, and that if he wanted to be there he must be in service.*

— * By passing the Bill, the Government conceded all the extravagant demands of the "Free" Staters; yet, a year later they took up arms against the Government.
—

Mr. J. A. P. Van der Merwe (Vredefort) deprecated sending the Bill to a Select Committee, arguing that the House itself should decide it. He referred to the difficulties experienced by farmers in the Free State. If a farmer refused to allow a Native to farm on the share system he simply refused to work. There were thousands of Natives on the farms there who hired ground and did little work. The farmers had to keep their children at home to do the work. Some of the Natives hired ground, did some sowing, then went to work in Johannesburg, and paid the owner of the farm half what he reaped from the harvest. That was not satisfactory. He was pleased to see the provisions the Minister proposed to make in this regard, and expressed the hope that the Native would only be tolerated among the whites as a labourer. The

Bill would meet what he considered a great want, and, as it was an urgent matter, he hoped the proposal for a Select Committee would not be agreed to.

Third Reading Debate.

Sir Lionel Phillips (Yeoville): But why should a Bill of this sort be brought before them now? The Government in the past had not been bashful in the appointing of Commissions, and one question he would ask was why, in this important matter, the Government had not appointed a Commission to take all the evidence and then come to the House with a measure which the House would have to approve of. Instead of that, they were cancelling the rights the Natives had in South Africa, and creating a very awkward hiatus between the time the Commission would be appointed and the time the Commission could define the areas which would be regarded as white areas and the areas which would be regarded as native areas. That was the one serious blot upon this measure.

He could see no justification, except that the hon. Minister, yielding to pressure from a certain section on that side of the House, had hastily brought on this measure. He thought from the speeches made in the House it was the consensus of opinion that Natives should not have farms in areas that were essentially white, just as it was desirable that white men should not be found in areas essentially native. And especially when they told the native population that they were taking away from them a right they had to-day, and they were going to substitute that right by appointing a Commission, they were giving them very little justification for being satisfied with this measure. He did not think they were going to gain anything by putting the cart before the horse. He did not know if Mr. Schreiner was accurate, but he told them that, roughly, in the Transvaal, where the matter was most acute, the Native population had bought something like 12,000 or 15,000 morgen of land in twelve years. That, he thought, showed there was no extreme urgency for the measure. To that extent he agreed entirely with the hon. member, and he believed the Minister would be well advised to send the Bill to a Select Committee, so that many of the details, which were extremely complicated and difficult, might be thrashed out in that atmosphere, rather than on the floor of the House. (Opposition cheers.)

Mr. E. N. *Grobler* (Edenburg) said: The present was one of the best measures that the Government had so far brought forward, and it appeared clear that they had a Government which truly represented the wishes of the public. It was impossible to delay the solution of the Native problem, and legislation on the subject had for a long time past been asked for.* At the same time, he did not entirely agree with the methods, proposed to be applied, and he did not like the system of allocating reserves for Natives. When once those reserves had been allocated, would it not result in injury to agriculture and cattle breeding? The farmers would suffer from lack of labour, and that deficiency would be a growing one. Neither could he agree to the principle of expropriation of land belonging to whites in order to increase the size of the native reserves. He considered the Bill was a complicated one. The matter should be settled by way of taxation, in the following way. All Natives who were in the service of whites should be exempted from taxation, and treated as well as possible, and other Natives should be encouraged to take similar service. There were enormous reserves where the Natives to pay a stiff tax. Then they would go and work for white people. The hon. member for Tembuland had offered many objections to the Bill. They should make that hon. member king of Tembuland. In a country of the blind a man with one eye would be king.

—

* By a "solution of the Native problem", "Free" State farmers generally mean the re-establishment of slavery.
subsequently formed General Botha's assurances to Mr. Harcourt.
See Chapter XVI. But some light is thrown on the subject
of these visionary Native Reserves by Mr. Fawcus' speech
based on official statistics (page 36 [above — last Fawcus quote]).

—

Mr. P. Duncan (Fordsburg) said he hoped the Minister would not take the view of the last speaker. Under the Bill it would be possible for farmers to accumulate on their land as many Natives as they could get, so long as they could use them as servants. (Labour cheers.) So far as he could see, even if it were carried out to the extent that it was proposed to go, it would not very much reduce the social contact which at present existed between whites and natives.

Sir W. B. Berry (Queenstown) said he would like to know why the Minister had run away from the Bill that had passed the second reading, and now tabled another Bill in the shape of many amendments. One would naturally complain that, seeing that they had in that House a Native Affairs Committee, a non-party committee, specially chosen to consider all matters relating to native affairs, that Bill, which was a most important matter and dealt with native affairs from A to Z, should have been referred to that committee. The same thing happened last session in reference to a Bill the Minister of Native Affairs kept on the paper until nearly the end of the session, and the House had to take the very unusual step almost on the last day of moving that committee proceedings on that Bill be taken that day six months. He (Sir W. B. Berry) proposed to move a similar amendment to the motion now before the House. In the remarks he addressed when the Bill came up for second reading he had ventured to say that there was no call for a bill of that nature at all; there was no need for a Bill revolutionizing the attitude of the Union with respect to the natives generally. The only clue they could get to the reason why the Bill was introduced was that a few die-hards on the other side of the House had given the Minister to understand that unless he brought in a Bill of that kind, or of a similarly drastic nature, the position of the Government was in danger. He hoped some of these die-hards would come forward that evening and tell them plainly and bluntly why they wanted that Bill, why they were going to thrust it on the country without any notice, and why they were calling on the House to revolutionize the whole tenour and the whole order of things in regard to land matters as far as the Natives were concerned. Proceeding, the hon. member said the only justification that had been offered for this Bill was that a large amount of land had been transferred from Europeans to

Natives. An analysis of the return, however, showed that only sixteen farms in the Transvaal had been so transferred during the last three years. Surely that was not any justification why the European people of the Union should get into a panic and why the administration of the day were seeking to place on the Statute Book this most drastic legislation. Another reason why he objected to this Bill was that it purported to appoint a Commission to investigate to what extent and in what parts and in what time land should be selected by the Commission for the purpose of being reserved as additional native areas within the Union. They were not given any guarantee that the Commission was going to be appointed nor any guarantee that it would ever report, but at the same time whilst these indefinite assurances were attempted to be given to the House there was no getting over this fact, that there was no time limit in the Bill by which the real enacting clause in the Bill was to have any cessation. When he spoke on this Bill before he supported it only on the understanding that a time limit was to be put in, or that it should be an annual Bill. He said unhesitatingly that the whole tendency of the Bill, as it stood at the second reading, and more especially as it stood with the amendments by the Minister on the notice paper, was to drive the Native peasant off the land. The only refuge that that Native had was the town.

The country had not been prepared in any way for a Bill of this kind. A cry had been heard throughout the land against the iniquities proposed in the Bill. If it had been found absolutely necessary that legislation of this kind should be introduced, the least that could be expected was that ample time should be given to the Natives to thoroughly acquire a knowledge of the contents of the measure. That opportunity had not been given them, and in this respect there was a very serious grievance. For the good order and peace of the Union there was a very great danger ahead. He had understood from those well versed in native affairs that one of the greatest dangers that could threaten us was to give the Natives anything in the shape of a common grievance. Divide and rule had been a wise precaution in the government of the Natives. When a common grievance was found by four or five million people one could understand how great that grievance must be. One amendment the Minister had put on the paper must give serious pause. The late Minister of Native Affairs issued to members last session a Squatters Bill. The greatest objection to that measure, and one which he thought led to its withdrawal, was that it proposed to remove thousands upon thousands of natives from land which they had been in the occupation of for scores of years. It was in consequence of the disturbance which that Bill caused throughout the Union that it was withdrawn. In one of the amendments on the paper the present Minister of Native Affairs brought back in a somewhat clandestine manner the most objectionable feature of the Bill that was withdrawn.

Mr. Speaker: The amendment is not yet before the House.

Sir W. B. *Berry*: What Bill is it then that is to go into Committee? (Hear, hear.) Is it the Bill which was read a second time or the Bill comprised in the Minister's amendments? He moved that the House go into committee on the Bill this day six months.

Mr. T. L. *Schreiner* (Tembuland), in seconding the amendment, said that sufficient notice had not been given of the provisions of the Bill, although the Natives, thanks to the time which had elapsed since the second reading, were better acquainted with the measure than they were a little while ago.

Mr. Schreiner proceeded to quote opinions from native newspapers on the Bill. The 'Tsala ea Batho', of Kimberley, said: "We are standing on the brink of the precipice. We appealed to certain members of Parliament against the suspension clause in Mr. Sauer's Land Bill, and the result of our appeal has been an agreement between Sir Thomas Smartt and the Minister to the effect that the first part of the Bill only be proceeded with. The effect of this agreement is infinitely worse than the whole Bill. In its entirety, there were certain saving clauses, one of them practically excluding the Cape Province from the operation of the Bill. Under the present agreement, all these clauses are dropped, and section 1 of the Bill, which prohibits the sale of land between Europeans and Natives (pending the report of a future Commission) is applicable to all parts of the Union, including the Cape Province. Now, then, if this suspension clause becomes law, what is going to happen? It is simply this: That the whole land policy of the Union of South Africa is the land policy of the Orange Free State, and it will be as difficult to abrogate that suspension as it is difficult to recall a bullet, once fired through some one's head, and resuscitate the victim. Our object then should be to prevent the pistol being fired off, as prevention is infinitely better than cure." One paper that he was quoting from was (Mr. Schreiner went on to say) pleased, because it believed that this Bill was going to Select Committee. There was another native paper, published in Natal, which acknowledged the efforts which the missionaries had made on behalf of the Natives in regard to this Bill. There was a native paper, published at Dundee, which said that, if the Bill were in the interests of the Natives, and the Government were actuated by a sincere regard for them, they would not have hesitated to publish it broadcast, instead of being in such haste to push the matter through the House.*

— * All efforts to induce the South African Government to circulate
translations of the Natives' Land Act among the Natives of the Union
have proved fruitless. — Author.
—

Mr. Schreiner (continuing) referred to the resolution passed by the Natal Missionary Conference, and the views expressed by the Chairman of the Transvaal Missionary Conference in opposition to the Bill. He mentioned that it had been decided in Johannesburg to call a meeting of missionary societies throughout the Union, to determine what action could be taken in case clause 1 was proceeded with. He had also received a telegram from the Witwatersrand Church Council, stating that a telegram had been sent to the Minister strongly protesting against section 1 being enacted before the proposed Commission had thoroughly investigated the whole question of alternative areas. Mr. Schreiner urged that, if they proceeded with this Bill, and passed clause 1 of the old Bill, and appointed a Commission, these restrictions with regard to purchase and sale, which the Natives had feared, and which the missionaries, on behalf of the Natives, feared and protested against, would become a fact. For that reason, he said they should rather put off the Bill.

Every one was feeling the pressure of their legislative duties. Was this the time, therefore, for passing a measure of such a far-reaching character, and where every clause demanded the most careful consideration and scrutiny? Was it the right thing because he had a majority at his back for the Minister to say that they must get this Bill through this session? He held that this was not right. It was not fair to those who had the solution of the question at heart. (Cheers.)

Sir E. H. *Walton* (Port Elizabeth, Central) said he entirely supported the amendment of the hon. member for Queen's Town. He had a telegram from a mass meeting of Natives held in Port Elizabeth, in which they hoped that the House would postpone decision on this question until the Commission had sat and reported. That seemed to him an entirely reasonable request, and it seemed all the more necessary that this should be done on account of the very large alterations that it had been found necessary to make in the Bill.

They had native protests from all parts of South Africa against this measure, and when one saw what was proposed in this Act, they could not wonder at these protests. (Hear, hear.) Therefore he put it that these protests should receive fair consideration from members on all sides of the House. Legislation of this kind was unfortunate from the point of view of the Natives. The more intelligent of the Natives in this country were asking for time. They said: "You are putting this thing upon us, give us time to consider it. Allow this Commission to get to work, allow this Commission to put before us the provisions you are going to make for us, and when this is done we will submit to anything that is fair." No man, and the Native was just a man like the rest of us, liked the old arrangements to be disturbed, because it upset him, and the Native might oppose it, because he was frightened. They must admit that they had not given the native leaders and chiefs an opportunity to come down to Cape Town and give their views. It was unfortunate that this measure had been more or less rushed. There was no mention of it in the Governor-General's speech, and therefore the Natives were not prepared for the consideration of the question.

Mr. M. *Alexander* (Cape Town, Castle) said he was still of opinion that a very dangerous principle was introduced in the Bill, especially so far as the Cape was concerned. In the speech delivered by the Governor-General at the opening of the session there was not the slightest reference to the present measure, which apparently had been brought in as an afterthought, and something must have occurred after the Governor-General's speech was delivered, otherwise one could not conceive of such an important Bill being omitted from the speech. As it was the Bill would simply hang things up until the Commission reported, and now the House would be legislating in the dark. The vast majority of Natives had declared themselves to be against the Bill. He had had no desire whatever that party capital should be made out of the measure — (hear, hear) — but he desired to see a measure which would bear the mark of statesmanship, and not of panic and hurry. Their Commission could report before next session, and then in the early stages of the session a Bill could be introduced and be adopted on its merits. In the interests of South Africa, in the interests of the Natives, and in the interests of just legislation let the Government withdraw the Bill, and appoint a Commission, and then justice and not injustice would be done. (Hear, hear.)

Dr. A. H. *Watkins* (Barkly) said that there was a tacit understanding that the Minister would refer this Bill, if he were not prepared to accept a purely temporary measure, to a Select Committee. During the three years of the Union Parliament every matter practically dealing with Natives had been brought before the Select Committee on Native Affairs and their opinion had been asked. For some reason, which it was difficult for him to understand, the Minister had not seen fit to carry out that course. Sixteen days had elapsed since the second reading of this Bill was taken on which the Select Committee could have sat morning after morning and dealt with the Bill.

The necessity of passing only a temporary measure instead of appearing to pass a measure which would permanently deal with this question, was more evident tonight than when they took the second reading.

Mr. H. M. *Meyler* (Weenen) said that he would support the motion of Sir Bisset Berry. He thought it would be a great injustice to the Natives, and especially the Natives of Natal, who really knew nothing of this measure, to force it through now. Since the second reading, his attention had been drawn to certain provisions in this Bill, which made it more dangerous still to hurry legislation, because he found that, although there was an exemption in the Bill as regarded agreements lawfully entered into, the vast majority of the agreements at present in force amongst the Natives of Natal were not strictly lawful, according to their Statute law. As they had no less than 380,000 Natives squatting on private lands in Natal, according to the Minister's own figures, it would be a fatal mistake to do anything to upset these people, until they had something ready to provide for them instead. The difficulty was that under the Natal law no oral contract was binding for more than twelve months, and many of those squatters had not got oral contracts, but were more or less on sufferance on the farms. It would be a great danger to pass legislation which would lead to the moving of a large portion of these people before they got an inch of land provided for their use. He objected to legislation being brought forward too hurriedly, and when they had got 4 1/2 millions of Natives, only an infinitesimal portion of whom could possibly know the nature of the Bill, and seeing that it affected them as well as the white population, they had a perfect right to have it explained to them by the Government officials and let their members of Parliament for the divisions in which they lived give their opinions on the question. That would take months, and it was impossible to get a proper opinion of the Natives until hon. members had been away from the House for some time. The Right Hon. the Prime Minister admitted they should stand as the guardians of the Natives, and admitted that they should go slowly, and he hoped the hon. Minister would be willing to reconsider the Bill and allow it to be put off, and let them have an interim report, at any rate, from the Commission, before they were asked to pass legislation in that matter. ==

The Bill was contested at every stage and numerous divisions were challenged. In each instance, the Speaker would put the Question, and the "steam-roller" would go to work with the inevitable result. The division lists ranged from 17 against 71 to 32 against 60, the majority in each case being in favour of repression. It would be just as well to give at least one of these division lists. The English names in the majority are those of some Natal members (Ministerialists) or representatives of purely Dutch constituencies: —

Division

Dr. A. H. Watkins (Barkly) called for a division, which was taken with the following result.

Ayes — 32.

Andrews, William Henry
Baxter, William Duncan
Berry, William Bisset
Blaine, George
Boydell, Thomas
Brown, Daniel Maclaren
Creswell, Frederic Hugh Page
Duncan, Patrick
Fawcus, Alfred
Fitzpatrick, James Percy
Henderson, James
Henwood, Charlie
Hunter, David
Jagger, John William
King, John Gavin
Long, Basil Kellett
Macaulay, Donald
Madeley, Walter Bayley
Meyler, Hugh Mowbray
Nathan, Emile
Oliver, Henry Alfred
Quinn, John William
Rockey, Willie
Runciman, William
Sampson, Henry William
Schreiner, Theophilus Lyndall
Searle, James
Smartt, Thomas William
Walton, Edgar Harris
Watkins, Arnold Hirst

Morris Alexander and J. Hewat tellers.

Noes — 57.

Alberts, Johannes Joachim
Becker, Heinrich Christian
Bosman, Hendrik Johannes
Botha, Louis
Brain, Thomas Phillip
Burton, Henry
Clayton, Walter Frederick
Cronje, Frederik Reinhardt
Currey, Henry Latham
De Beer, Michiel Johannes
De Jager, Andries Lourens
De Waal, Hendrik
Du Toit, Gert Johan Wilhelm
Geldenhuys, Lourens
Graaff, David Pieter de Villiers
Griffin, William Henry
Grobler, Evert Nicolaas
Grobler, Pieter Gert Wessel
Joubert, Christiaan Johannes Jacobus
Joubert, Jozua Adriaan
Keyter, Jan Garhard
Kuhn, Pieter Gysbert
Lemmer, Lodewyk Arnoldus Slabbert
Maasdorp, Gysbert Henry
Malan, Francois Stephanus
Marais, Johannes Henoch
Marais, Pieter Gerhardus
Merriman, John Xavier
Meyer, Izaak Johannes
Myburgh, Marthinus Wilhelmus
Neethling, Andrew Murray
Neser, Johannes Adriaan
Nicholson, Richard Granville
Oothuisen, Ockert Almero
Orr, Thomas
Rademeyer, Jacobus Michael
Sauer, Jacobus Wilhelmus
Serfontein, Hendrik Philippus
Smuts, Jan Christiaan
Smuts, Tobias
Steyl, Johannes Petrus Gerhardus
Steytler, George Louis
Theron, Hendrik Schalk
Theron, Petrus Jacobus George
Van der Merwe, Johannes Adolph P.
Van der Walt, Jacobus

Van Eeden, Jacobus Willem
Van Heerden, Hercules Christian
Venter, Jan Abraham
Vermaas, Hendrik Cornelius Wilhelmus
Vintcent, Alwyn Ignatius
Vosloo, Johannes Arnoldus
Watt, Thomas
Wilcocks, Carl Theodorus Muller
Wiltshire, Henry

H. Mentz and G. A. Louw, tellers.

Chapter III The Natives' Land Act

I blush to think that His Majesty's representative signed a law like this,
and signed it in such circumstances.
Rev. Amos Burnet
(Chairman and General Superintendent of
the Transvaal and Swazieland District,
Wesleyan Methodist Church).

Up to now we have dealt with the history of the Land Act from its commencement, and all the speeches and official documents we have mentioned hitherto say nothing about restricting Europeans in their ownership of land. And no matter what other principles one might read into the Act, it would be found that the principles underlying it were those of extending the "Free" State land laws throughout the Union — an extension by which Natives would be prohibited from investing their earnings in land whereon they could end their days in peace.

There seems to be good reason for believing that the Government were advised, by the legal advisers of the Crown, that the Natives' Land Bill would be class legislation of a kind that would never be allowed by His Majesty's Government. The originators of the Bill, however, were determined so to circumvent the constitutional quibble raised by the legal advisers as to seal our doom; and by adroitly manipulating its legal phrases, it seems that it was recasted in such a manner as to give it a semblance of a paper restriction on European encroachment on native rights. But class legislation the Act is, for whereas in his travels about South Africa, since the passing of this Act, the author has met many a native family with their stock, turned out by the Act upon the roads, he never met one white man so hounded by the same Act, and debarred from living where he pleased.

The squatters form a particular section of the community specifically affected by the Land Act; and there is no such person in South Africa as a white squatter. Although it is insistently affirmed that the law applies both to Europeans and Natives, the conclusion cannot be avoided that it is directed exclusively against the Native. This is the naked truth that turns all other explanations of the fact into mere shuffling and juggling. And the reader will find that in Section 11, at the end of the statute which is here reproduced (whether the omission of Europeans was a mistake of the Parliamentary draftsmen, or the printers, we know not), it is expressly stated that "this Act may be cited for all purposes as the *natives*' Land Act, 1913." Who, then, will continue to argue that it was intended for Europeans as well?

== No. 27, 1913.]

Act
to
Make further provision as to the purchase and leasing of Land
by Natives and other Persons in the several parts of the Union and for

other purposes in connection with the ownership and occupation of Land by Natives and other Persons.

Be it enacted by the King's Most Excellent Majesty, the Senate and the House of Assembly of the Union of South Africa, as follows: —

1. (1) From and after the commencement of this Act, land outside the scheduled native areas shall, until Parliament, acting upon the report of the commission appointed under this Act, shall have made other provision, be subjected to the following provisions, that is to say: —

Except with the approval of the Governor-General —

(a) a native shall not enter into any agreement or transaction for the purchase, hire, or other acquisition from a person other than a native, of any such land or of any right thereto, interest therein, or servitude thereover; and

(b) a person other than a native shall not enter into any agreement or transaction for the purchase, hire, or other acquisition from a native of any such land or of any right thereto, interest therein, or servitude thereover.

(2) From and after the commencement of this Act, no person other than a native shall purchase, hire or in any other manner whatever acquire any land in a scheduled native area or enter into any agreement or transaction for the purchase, hire or other acquisition, direct or indirect, of any such land or of any right thereto or interest therein or servitude thereover, except with the approval of the Governor-General.

(3) A statement showing the number of approvals granted by the Governor-General under sub-sections (1) and (2) of this section and giving the names and addresses of the persons to whom such approvals were granted, the reasons for granting the same, and the situation of the lands in respect of which they were granted, shall, within six weeks after the commencement of each ordinary session of Parliament, be laid upon the Tables of both Houses of Parliament.

(4) Every agreement or any other transaction whatever entered into in contravention of this section shall be null and void ab initio.

2. (1) As soon as may be after the commencement of this Act the Governor-General shall appoint a commission whose functions shall be to inquire and report —

(a) what areas should be set apart as areas within which natives shall not be permitted to acquire or hire land or interests in land;

(b) what areas should be set apart as areas within which persons other than natives shall not be permitted to acquire or hire land or interests in land.

The commission shall submit with any such report —

(i) descriptions of the boundaries of any area which it proposes should be so set apart; and

(ii) a map or maps showing every such area.

(2) The commission shall proceed with and complete its inquiry and present its reports and recommendations to the Minister within two years after the commencement of this Act, and may present *interim* reports and recommendations: Provided that Parliament may by resolution extend (if necessary) the time for the completion of the commission's inquiry. All such reports and recommendations shall be laid by the Minister, as soon as possible after the receipt thereof, upon the Tables of both Houses of Parliament.

3. (1) The commission shall consist of not less than five persons, and if any member of the commission die or resign or, owing to absence or any other reason, is unable to act, his place shall be filled by the Governor-General.

(2) The commission may delegate to any of its members the carrying out of any part of an inquiry which under this Act it is appointed to hold and may appoint persons to assist it or to act as assessors thereto or with any members thereof delegated as aforesaid, and may regulate its own procedure.

(3) The reports and recommendations of the majority of the commission shall be deemed to be the reports and recommendations of the commission: Provided that any recommendations of any member who dissents from the majority of the commission shall, if signed by him, be included in any such report aforesaid.

(4) The commission or any member thereof or any person acting as assistant, or assessor, or secretary thereto may enter upon any land for the purposes of its inquiries and obtain thereon the information necessary to prosecute the inquiries. The commission shall without fee or other charge have access to the records and registers relating to land in any public office or in the office of any divisional council or other local authority.

4. (1) For the purposes of establishing any such area as is described in section *two*, the Governor-General may, out of moneys which Parliament may vote for the purpose, acquire any land or interest in land.

(2) In default of agreement with the owners of the land or the holders of interests therein the provisions of the law in force in the Province in which such land or

interest in land is situate relating to the expropriation of land for public purposes shall apply and, if in any Province there be no such law, the provisions of Proclamation No. 5 of 1902 of the Transvaal and any amendment thereof shall mutatis mutandis apply.

5. (1) Any person who is a party to any attempted purchase, sale, hire or lease, or to any agreement or transaction which is in contravention of this Act or any regulation made thereunder shall be guilty of an offence and liable on conviction to a fine not exceeding one hundred pounds or, in default of payment, to imprisonment with or without hard labour for a period not exceeding six months, and if the act constituting the offence be a continuing one, the offender shall be liable to a further fine not exceeding five pounds for every day which that act continues.

(2) In the event of such an offence being committed by a company, corporation, or other body of persons (not being a firm or partnership), every director, secretary, or manager of such company, corporation, or body who is within the Union shall be liable to prosecution and punishment and, in the event of any such offence being committed by a firm or partnership, every member of the firm or partnership who is within the Union shall be liable to prosecution and punishment.

6. In so far as the occupation by natives of land outside the scheduled native areas may be affected by this Act, the provisions thereof shall be construed as being in addition to and not in substitution for any law in force at the commencement thereof relating to such occupation; but in the event of a conflict between the provisions of this Act and the provisions of any such law, the provisions of this Act shall, save as is specially provided therein, prevail:

Provided that —

(a) nothing in any such law or in this Act shall be construed
as restricting the number of natives who, as farm labourers,
may reside on any farm in the Transvaal;

(b) in any proceedings for a contravention of this Act
the burden of proving that a native is a farm labourer
shall be upon the accused;

(c) until Parliament, acting upon the report of the said commission,
has made other provision, no native resident on any farm
in the Transvaal or Natal shall be liable to penalties
or to be removed from such farm under any law,
if at the commencement of this Act he or the head of his family
is registered for taxation or other purposes
in the department of Native Affairs as being resident on such farm,
nor shall the owner of any such farm be liable to the penalties
imposed by section *five* in respect of the occupation of the land
by such native; but nothing herein contained shall affect any right

possessed by law by an owner or lessee of a farm to remove any native therefrom.

7. (1) Chapter XXXIV of the Orange Free State Law Book and Law No. 4 of 1895 of the Orange Free State shall remain of full force and effect, subject to the modifications and interpretations in this section provided, and sub-section (1) (a) of the next succeeding section shall not apply to the Orange Free State.

(2) Those heads of families, with their families, who are described in article *twenty* of Law No. 4 of 1895 of the Orange Free State shall in the circumstances described in that article be deemed to fall under the provisions of Ordinance No. 7 of 1904 of that Province or of any other law hereafter enacted amending or substituted for that Ordinance.

(3) Whenever in Chapter XXXIV of the Orange Free State Law Book the expressions "lease" and "leasing" are used, those expressions shall be construed as including or referring to an agreement or arrangement whereby a person, in consideration of his being permitted to occupy land, renders or promises to render to any person a share of the produce thereof, or any valuable consideration of any kind whatever other than his own labour or services or the labour or services of any of his family.

8. (1) Nothing in this Act contained shall be construed as, —

(a) preventing the continuation or renewal (until Parliament acting upon the report of the said commission has made other provision) of any agreement or arrangement lawfully entered into and in existence at the commencement of this Act which is a hiring or leasing of land as defined in this Act; or

(b) invalidating or affecting in any manner whatever any agreement or any other transaction for the purchase of land lawfully entered into prior to the commencement of this Act, or as prohibiting any person from purchasing at any sale held by order of a competent court any land which was hypothecated by a mortgage bond passed before the commencement of this Act; or

(c) prohibiting the acquisition at any time of land or interests in land by devolution or succession on death, whether under a will or on intestacy; or

(d) preventing the due registration in the proper deeds office (whenever registration is necessary) of documents giving effect to any such agreement, transaction, devolution or succession as is in this section mentioned; or

(e) prohibiting any person from claiming, acquiring,
or holding any such servitude as under Chapter VII,
of the Irrigation and Conservation of Waters Act, 1912,
he is specially entitled to claim, acquire, or hold; or

(f) in any way altering the law in force at the commencement of this Act
relating to the acquisition of rights to minerals,
precious or base metals or precious stones; or

(g) applying to land within the limits in which a municipal council,
town council, town board, village management board,
or health committee or other local authority
exercises jurisdiction; or

(h) applying to land held at the commencement of the Act by any society
carrying on, with the approval of the Governor-General,
educational or missionary work amongst natives; or

(i) prohibiting the acquisition by natives from any person whatever
of land or interests in land in any township lawfully established
prior to the commencement of this Act, provided it is
a condition of the acquisition that no land or interest in land
in such township has at any time been or shall in future be,
transferred except to a native or coloured person; or

(j) permitting the alienation of land or its diversion from
the purposes for which it was set apart if, under section
one hundred and forty-seven of the South African Act, 1909,
or any other law, such land could not be alienated or so diverted
except under the authority of an Act of Parliament; or

(k) in any way modifying the provisions of any law whereby
mortgages of or charges over land may be created
to secure advances out of public moneys for specific purposes
mentioned in such law and the interest of such advances,
or whereunder the mortgagee or person having the charge
may enter and take possession of the land so mortgaged or charged
except that in any sale of such land in accordance with such law
the provisions of this Act shall be observed.

(2) Nothing in this Act contained which imposes restrictions upon the acquisition by any person of land or right thereto, interests therein, or servitudes thereover, shall be in force in the Province of the Cape of Good Hope, if and for so long as such person would, by such restrictions, be prevented from acquiring or holding a qualification whereunder he is or may become entitled to be registered as a voter at parliamentary elections in any electoral division in the said Province.

9. The Governor-General may make regulations for preventing the overcrowding of huts and other dwellings in the stadts, native villages and settlements and other places in which natives are congregated in areas not under the jurisdiction of any local authority, the sanitation of such places and for the maintenance of the health of the inhabitants thereof.

10. In this Act, unless inconsistent with the context, —

"scheduled native area" shall mean any area described in the Schedule to this Act;

"native" shall mean any person, male or female, who is a member of an aboriginal race or tribe of Africa; and shall further include any company or other body of persons, corporate or unincorporate, if the persons who have a controlling interest therein are natives;

"interest in land" shall include, in addition to other interest in land, the interest which a mortgagee of, or person having charge over, land acquires under a mortgage bond or charge;

"Minister" shall mean the Minister of Native Affairs;

"farm labourer" shall mean a native who resides on a farm and is bona fide, but not necessarily continuously employed by the owner or lessee thereof in domestic service or in farming operations:

Provided that —

(a) if such native reside on one farm and is employed
on another farm of the same owner or lessee he shall be deemed
to have resided, and to have been employed, on one and the same farm;

(b) such native shall not be deemed to be bona fide employed
unless he renders ninety days' service at least
in one calendar year on the farm occupied by the owner or lessee
or on another farm of the owner or lessee and no rent is paid
or valuable consideration of any kind, other than service,
is given by him to the owner or lessee in respect of residence
on such farm or farms.

A person shall be deemed for the purposes of this Act to hire land if, in consideration of his being permitted to occupy that land or any portion thereof —

(a) he pays or promises to pay to any person a rent in money; or

(b) he renders or promises to render to any person a share of the produce of that land, or any valuable consideration of any kind whatever other than his own labour or services or the labour or services of his family.

11. This Act may be cited for all purposes as the Natives' Land Act, 1913. ==

The foregoing result of a legislative jumble is "the law", and this law, like Alexander the coppersmith, "hath done us much harm". Mr. Sauer carried his Bill less by reason than by sheer force of numbers, and partly by promises which he afterwards broke. Among these broken promises was the definite assurance he gave Parliament that the Bill would be referred to the Select Committee on Native Affairs, so that the Natives, who are not represented in Parliament, their European friends and the Missionary bodies on behalf of the Natives, could be able at the proper time to appear before this committee and state any objection which they might have to the Bill. But when that time came, the Minister flatly refused to refer it to the committee. This change of front is easily explained, because the weight of evidence which could have been given before any Parliamentary committee would have imperilled the passage of the Bill.

As might have been expected, the debate on the Bill created the greatest alarm amongst the native population, for they had followed its course with the keenest interest. Nothing short of a declaration of war against them could have created a similar excitement, although the hope was entertained in some quarters, that a body of men like the Ministerialists in Parliament (a majority of whom are never happier than when attesting the Christian character of their race) would in course of days attend the Holy Communion, remember the 11th Commandment, and do unto others as they would that men should do unto them. Our people, in fact a number of them, said amongst themselves that even Dutchmen sing Psalms — all the Psalms, including the 24th; and, believing as they did that Dutchmen could have no other religion besides the one recommended in the New Testament and preached by the predikants of the Dutch Reformed Church, were prepared to commend their safety to the influence of that sweet and peaceable religion. However, some other Natives, remembering what took place before the South African war, took a different view of these religious incidents. Those Natives, especially of the old Republics, knew that the only dividing fence between the Transvaal Natives and complete slavery was the London Convention; they, therefore, now that the London Convention in fact had ceased to exist, had evil forebodings regarding the average Republican's treatment of the Natives, which was seldom influenced by religious scruples, and they did not hesitate to express their fears.

Personally we must say that if any one had told us at the beginning of 1913, that a majority of members of the Union Parliament were capable of passing a law like the Natives' Land Act, whose object is to prevent the Natives from ever rising above the position of servants to the whites, we would have regarded that person as a fit subject for the lunatic asylum. But the passing of that Act and its operation have rudely forced the fact upon us that the Union Parliament is capable of producing any measure that is subversive of native interests; and that the complete arrest of native progress is the object aimed at in their efforts to include the Protectorates in their Union. Thus we think that their sole reason for seeking to incorporate Basutoland, Swaziland and Bechuanaland is that, when they have definitely eliminated the Imperial factor from South Africa, as they are unmistakably trying to do, they may have a million more slaves than if the Protectorates were excluded.

In this connexion, the realization of the prophecy of an old Basuto became increasingly believable to us. It was to this effect, namely: "That the Imperial Government, after conquering the Boers, handed back to them their old Republics, and a nice little present in the shape of the Cape Colony and Natal — the two English Colonies. That the Boers are now ousting the Englishmen from the public service, and when they have finished with them, they will make a law declaring it a crime for a Native to live in South Africa, unless he is a servant in the employ of a Boer, and that from this it will be just one step to complete slavery." This is being realized, for to-day we have, extended throughout the Union of South Africa, a "Free" State law which makes it illegal for Natives to live on farms except as servants in the employ of Europeans. There is another "Free" State law, under which no Native may live in a municipal area or own property in urban localities. He can only live in town as a servant in the employ of a European. And if the followers of General Hertzog are permitted to dragoon the Union Government into enforcing "Free" State ideals against the Natives of the Union, as they have successfully done under the Natives' Land Act, it will only be a matter of time before we have a Natives' Urban Act enforced throughout South Africa. Then we will have the banner of slavery fully unfurled (of course, under another name) throughout the length and breadth of the land.

When the Natives' Land Bill was before Parliament, meetings were held in many villages and locations in protest against the Ministerial surrender to the Republicans, of which the Bill was the outcome. At the end of March, 1913, the Native National Congress met in Johannesburg, and there a deputation was appointed to go to Capetown and point out to the Government some, at least, of the harm that would follow legislation of the character mapped out in Parliament on February 28 when the Land Act was first announced. They were to urge that such a measure would be exploitation of the cruelest kind, that it would not only interfere with the economic independence of the Natives, but would reduce them for ever to a state of serfdom, and degrade them as nothing has done since slavery was abolished at the Cape. Missionaries also, and European friends of the Natives, did not sit still. Resolution after resolution, telegraphic and other representations, were made to Mr. Sauer, from meetings in various parts of the country, counselling prudence. Even such societies as the Transvaal Landowners, who had long been crying for a measure to separate whites from blacks, and vice versa, urged that the Bill should not be passed during the same session in which it was introduced, that the country should be given an opportunity to digest it, in order, if necessary, to suggest amendments. The Missionary bodies, too, represent a following of Natives numbering hundreds of thousands of souls, on whose behalf they pleaded for justice. These bodies urged that before passing a law, prohibiting the sale and lease of land to Natives, and expelling squatters from their homes, the Government should provide locations to which the evicted Natives could go. But all these representations made no impression upon the Government, who, instead, preferred to act upon the recommendation of thirteen diminutive petitions (signed in all by 304 Dutchmen in favour of the Bill)* than to be guided by the overwhelming weight of public opinion that was against its passage. Thus it became clear that the Native's position in his own country was not an enviable one, for once a law was made prohibiting the sale of landed property to Natives, it would be almost impossible to get a South African Parliament to amend it.

— * One of these thirteen petitions had only four signatures, which was but one better than that of the Tooley Street tailors.
—

The Government, which at the beginning assured Parliament of their humane intentions, proceeded to delete the mildest clauses of the measure and to insert some very harsh ones; and almost each time that the Bill came before the House, one or two fresh drastic clauses were added. But it is comforting to note that even Parliament was not entirely satisfied with this, its heroic piece of legislation. Thus Mr. Meyler of Natal did, as only a lawyer could with a view to recasting the Bill, some very useful work in pointing out the possible harm with which the Bill was fraught. We wish that his clever speeches and observations (much of which have come true), might yet be sifted out of the big Parliamentary Reports, and published in a concise little pamphlet.

Sir David Hunter, another member of Natal, expressed himself as follows: —

== While every one seemed animated with a desire to do what was right and just to the Natives, there was a feeling that certain of the details of the measure required amendment. He was more than pleased when the Minister closed the debate by a speech in which he seemed to be willing to meet the wishes of those in the House who thought that amendment was required. He could not have imagined that the Bill would develop into the shape into which it had developed, and had he known that so great an alteration would take place in the general effect of the measure from what was foreshadowed by the hon. Minister when he had made that interesting speech on the second reading he (the speaker) could not have conscientiously voted for the second reading. He would have been better pleased had a resolution been taken not to bring in a Bill until the Commission had reported. That was the position he had taken up all through and he would much rather now that the matter should be dealt with in that way. If, however, the Bill was to be pressed through there should be guarantees in it which should allay all suspicion. Anything affecting the native people required to be done gradually and should be placed before them a long time before the change took place. He hoped there would yet be some steps taken to give them a greater sense of security. To give some idea of the feeling in the minds of the Natives he read a letter from a gentleman in Natal, largely interested in the Natives, which had expressed the opinion that the Natives stood uncompromisingly against any change in their present status until the Commission had reported. He hoped the hon. Minister would even yet endeavour to do something to meet their views.

Mr. C. H. Haggar (Roodepoort) said that from the point of those who had worked successfully in turning the uncivilized man into the civilized man the Bill was bound to be a failure. It was necessary not only to have legislation theoretically just, but also practically right and good. But there were many who felt that so far from the effect of that Bill being good it would be disastrous to a very large extent. The great sin which they had been committing was that they had always been legislating ahead of the people, and there had not been sufficient preparation for the changes which were proposed in that Bill; the Natives were not ready for it. The hon. member for Victoria West had said that there was a disposition in certain directions to repress the Natives. He (the speaker) believed that there was a feeling that white men had some divine right to the labour of the black, that the black people were to be hewers of wood and drawers of water, and he wanted to say that while men were obsessed with that feeling they would never be able to legislate fairly. They had no more divine right to the labour of the black people than they had to the labour of the white. To his mind the great point was, should their policy be one of repression or a policy of inspiration? They had inspired the Natives to a certain extent, but no sooner had they created an appetite than they had told the Natives they should go no further. Their policy was the policy of Tantalus. That Bill would create a feeling of insecurity in the minds of the Natives. There were those who said that if the Natives would not submit to dictation they should be wiped out. But that should not be their policy. They must cease the policy of repression and let it be one of wide inspiration. ==

But alas! these and similar pleadings had about as much effect upon the Ministerial steam-roller as the proverbial water on a duck's back. With a rush the Natives' Land Bill was dispatched from the Lower House to the Senate, adopted hurriedly by the Senate, returned to the Lower House, and went at the same pace to Government House, and there receiving the Governor-General's signature, it immediately became law. As regards the Governor-General's signature, His Excellency, if Ministers are to be believed, was ready to sign the Bill (or rather signified his intention of doing so) long before it was introduced into Parliament. This excited haste suggests grave misgivings as to the character of the Bill. Why all the hurry and scurry, and why the Governor-General's approval in advance? Other Bills are passed and approved by the Governor, yet they do not come into operation until some given day — the beginning of the next calendar year, or of the next financial year. But the Natives' Land Act became law and was operating as soon as it could be promulgated.

After desperately protesting, with individual members of Parliament and with Cabinet Ministers, and getting nothing for their pains, the delegates from the Native Congress wrote Lord Gladstone, from an office about two hundred yards distant from Government House, requesting His Excellency to withhold his assent to the Natives' Land Bill until the people mostly concerned (i.e. the Natives) had had a chance of making known to His Majesty the King their objection to the measure. His Excellency replied that such a course "was not within his constitutional functions." Thereby the die was cast, and the mandate went forth that the land laws of the Orange "Free" State, which is commonly known as "the Only Slave State", shall be the laws of the whole Union of South Africa. The worst feature in the case is the fact that, even with the Governments of the late Republics, the Presidents always had the power to exempt some Natives from the operation of those laws, and that prerogative had been liberally used by successive Presidents. Now, however, without a President, and with the prerogative of the King (by the exercise of which the evils of such a law could have been averted) disowned by the King's own Ministers on the spot, God in the heavens alone knows what will become of the hapless, because voteless, Natives, who are without a President, "without a King", and with a Governor-General without constitutional functions, under task-masters whose national traditions are to enslave the dark races.

Chapter IV One Night with the Fugitives

Es ist unkoeniglich zu weinen — ach,
Und hier nicht weinen ist unvaeterlich.
Schiller.

"Pray that your flight be not in winter," said Jesus Christ; but it was only during the winter of 1913 that the full significance of this New Testament passage was revealed to us. We left Kimberley by the early morning train during the first week in July, on a tour of observation regarding the operation of the Natives' Land Act; and we arrived at Bloemhof, in Transvaal, at about noon. On the River Diggings there were no actual cases representing the effects of the Act, but traces of these effects were everywhere manifest. Some fugitives of the Natives' Land Act had crossed the river in full flight. The fact that they reached the diggings a fortnight before our visit would seem to show that while the debates were proceeding in Parliament some farmers already viewed with eager eyes the impending opportunity for at once making slaves of their tenants and appropriating their stock; for, acting on the powers conferred on them by an Act signed by Lord Gladstone, so lately as June 16, they had during that very week (probably a couple of days after, and in some cases, it would seem, a couple of days before the actual signing of the Bill) approached their tenants with stories about a new Act which makes it criminal for any one to have black tenants and lawful to have black servants. Few of these Natives, of course, would object to be servants, especially if the white man is worth working for, but this is where the shoe pinches: one of the conditions is that the black man's (that is the servant's) cattle shall henceforth work for the landlord free of charge. Then the Natives would decide to leave the farm rather than make the landlord a present of all their life's savings, and some of them had passed through the diggings in search of a place in the Transvaal. But the higher up they went the more gloomy was their prospect as the news about the new law was now penetrating every part of the country.

One farmer met a wandering native family in the town of Bloemhof a week before our visit. He was willing to employ the Native and many more homeless families as follows: A monthly wage of 2 Pounds 10s. for each such family, the husband working in the fields, the wife in the house, with an additional 10s. a month for each son, and 5s. for each daughter, but on condition that the Native's cattle were also handed over to work for him. It must be clearly understood, we are told that the Dutchman added, that occasionally the Native would have to leave his family at work on the farm, and go out with his wagon and his oxen to earn money whenever and wherever he was told to go, in order that the master may be enabled to pay the stipulated wage. The Natives were at first inclined to laugh at the idea of working for a master with their families and goods and chattels, and then to have the additional pleasure of paying their own small wages, besides bringing money to pay the "Baas" for employing them. But the Dutchman's serious demeanour told them that his suggestion was "no joke". He himself had for some time been in need of a native cattle owner, to assist him as transport rider between Bloemhof, Mooifontein, London, and other diggings, in return for the occupation and cultivation of some of his waste lands in the district, but that was now illegal. He could only "employ" them; but, as he had no money to pay wages, their cattle would have to go out and earn it for him. Had they not heard of the law before? he inquired. Of course they had; in fact that is why they left the other place, but as they thought that it was but a "Free" State law, they took the anomalous situation for one of the multifarious aspects of the freedom of the "Free" State whence they came; they had scarcely thought that the Transvaal was similarly afflicted.

Needless to say the Natives did not see their way to agree with such a one-sided bargain. They moved up country, but only to find the next farmer offering the same terms, however, with a good many more disturbing details — and the next farmer and the next — so that after this native farmer had wandered from farm to farm, occasionally getting into trouble for travelling with unknown stock, "across my ground without my permission", and at times escaping arrest for he knew not what, and further, being abused for the crimes of having a black skin and no master, he sold some of his stock along the way, beside losing many which died of cold and starvation; and after thus having lost much of his substance, he eventually worked his way back to Bloemhof with the remainder, sold them for anything they could fetch, and went to work for a digger.

The experience of another native sufferer was similar to the above, except that instead of working for a digger he sold his stock for a mere bagatelle, and left with his family by the Johannesburg night train for an unknown destination. More native families crossed the river and went inland during the previous week, and as nothing had since been heard of them, it would seem that they were still wandering somewhere, and incidentally becoming well versed in the law that was responsible for their compulsory unsettlement.

Well, we knew that this law was as harsh as its instigators were callous, and we knew that it would, if passed, render many poor people homeless, but it must be confessed that we were scarcely prepared for such a rapid and widespread crash as it caused in the lives of the Natives in this neighbourhood. We left our luggage the next morning with the local Mission School teacher, and crossed the river to find out some more about this wonderful law of extermination. It was about 10 a.m. when we landed on the south bank of the Vaal River — the picturesque Vaal River, upon whose banks a hundred miles farther west we spent the best and happiest days of our boyhood. It was interesting to walk on one portion of the banks of that beautiful river — a portion which we had never traversed except as an infant in mother's arms more than thirty years before. How the subsequent happy days at Barkly West, so long past, came crowding upon our memory! — days when there were no railways, no bridges, and no system of irrigation. In rainy seasons, which at that time were far more regular and certain, the river used to overflow its high banks and flood the surrounding valleys to such an extent, that no punt could carry the wagons across. Thereby the transport service used to be hung up, and numbers of wagons would congregate for weeks on both sides of the river until the floods subsided. At such times the price of fresh milk used to mount up to 1s. per pint. There being next to no competition, we boys had a monopoly over the milk trade. We recalled the number of haversacks full of bottles of milk we youngsters often carried to those wagons, how we returned with empty bottles and with just that number of shillings. Mother and our elder brothers had leather bags full of gold and did not care for the "boy's money"; and unlike the boys of the neighbouring village, having no sisters of our own, we gave away some of our money to fair cousins, and jingled the rest in our pockets. We had been told from boyhood that sweets were injurious to the teeth, and so spurning these delights we had hardly any use for money, for all we wanted to eat, drink and wear was at hand in plenty. We could then get six or eight shillings every morning from the pastime of washing that number of bottles, filling them with fresh milk and carrying them down to the wagons; there was always such an abundance of the liquid that our shepherd's hunting dog could not possibly miss what we took, for while the flocks were feeding on the luscious buds of the haak-doorns and the orange-coloured blossoms of the rich mimosa and other wild vegetation that abounded on the banks of the Vaal River, the cows, similarly engaged, were gathering more and more milk.

The gods are cruel, and one of their cruellest acts of omission was that of giving us no hint that in very much less than a quarter of a century all those hundreds of heads of cattle, and sheep and horses belonging to the family would vanish like a morning mist, and that we ourselves would live to pay 30s. per month for a daily supply of this same precious fluid, and in very limited quantities. They might have warned us that Englishmen would agree with Dutchmen to make it unlawful for black men to keep milch cows of their own on the banks of that river, and gradually have prepared us for the shock.

Crossing the river from the Transvaal side brings one into the Province of the Orange "Free" State, in which, in the adjoining division of Boshof, we were born thirty-six years back. We remember the name of the farm, but not having been in this neighbourhood since infancy, we could not tell its whereabouts, nor could we say whether the present owner was a Dutchman, his lawyer, or a Hebrew merchant; one thing we do know, however: it is that even if we had the money and the owner was willing to sell the spot upon which we first saw the light of day and breathed the pure air of heaven, the sale would be followed with a fine of one hundred pounds. The law of the country forbids the sale of land to a Native. Russia is one of the most abused countries in the world, but it is extremely doubtful if the statute book of that Empire contains a law debarring the peasant from purchasing the land whereon he was born, or from building a home wherein he might end his days.

At this time we felt something rising from our heels along our back, gripping us in a spasm, as we were cycling along; a needlelike pang, too, pierced our heart with a sharp thrill. What was it? We remembered feeling something nearly like it when our father died eighteen years ago; but at that time our physical organs were fresh and grief was easily thrown off in tears, but then we lived in a happy South Africa that was full of pleasant anticipations, and now — what changes for the worse have we undergone! For to crown all our calamities, South Africa has by law ceased to be the home of any of her native children whose skins are dyed with a pigment that does not conform with the regulation hue.

We are told to forgive our enemies and not to let the sun go down upon our wrath, so we breathe the prayer that peace may be to the white races, and that they, including our present persecutors of the Union Parliament, may never live to find themselves deprived of all occupation and property rights in their native country as is now the case with the Native. History does not tell us of any other continent where the Bantu lived besides Africa, and if this systematic ill-treatment of the Natives by the colonists is to be the guiding principle of Europe's scramble for Africa, slavery is our only alternative; for now it is only as serfs that the Natives are legally entitled to live here. Is it to be thought that God is using the South African Parliament to hound us out of our ancestral homes in order to quicken our pace heavenward? But go from where to heaven? In the beginning, we are told, God created heaven and earth, and peopled the earth, for people do not shoot up to heaven from nowhere. They must have had an earthly home. Enoch, Melchizedek, Elijah, and other saints, came to heaven from earth. God did not say to the Israelites in their bondage: "Cheer up, boys; bear it all in good part for I have bright mansions on high awaiting you all." But he said: "I have surely seen the affliction of my people which are in Egypt, and have heard their cry by reason of their taskmasters; for I know their sorrows, and I am come down to bring them out of the hands of the Egyptians, and to bring them up out of that land unto a good land and a large, unto a land flowing with milk and honey." And He used Moses to carry out the promise He made to their ancestor Abraham in Canaan, that "unto thy seed will I give this land." It is to be hoped that in the Boer churches, entrance to which is barred against coloured people during divine service, they also read the Pentateuch.

It is doubtful if we ever thought so much on a single bicycle ride as we did on this journey; however, the sight of a policeman ahead of us disturbed these meditations and gave place to thoughts of quite another kind, for — we had no pass. Dutchmen, Englishmen, Jews, Germans, and other foreigners may roam the "Free" State without permission — but not Natives. To us it would mean a fine and imprisonment to be without a pass. The "pass" law was first instituted to check the movement of livestock over sparsely populated areas. In a sense it was a wise provision, in that it served to identify the livestock which one happened to be driving along the high road, to prove the bona fides of the driver and his title to the stock. Although white men still steal large droves of horses in Basutoland and sell them in Natal or in East Griqualand, they, of course, are not required to carry any passes. These white horse-thieves, to escape the clutches of the police, employ Natives to go and sell the stolen stock and write the passes for these Natives, forging the names of Magistrates and Justices of the Peace. Such native thieves in some instances ceasing to be hirelings in the criminal business, trade on their own, but it is not clear what purpose it is intended to serve by subjecting native pedestrians to the degrading requirement of carrying passes when they are not in charge of any stock.

In a few moments the policeman was before us and we alighted in presence of the representative of the law, with our feet on the accursed soil of the district in which we were born. The policeman stopped. By his looks and his familiar "Dag jong" we noticed that the policeman was Dutch, and the embodiment of affability. He spoke and we were glad to notice that he had no intention of dragging an innocent man to prison. We were many miles from the nearest police station, and in such a case one is generally able to gather the real views of the man on patrol, as distinct from the written code of his office, but our friend was becoming very companionable. Naturally we asked him about the operation of the plague law. He was a Transvaaler, he said, and he knew that Kafirs were inferior beings, but they had rights, and were always left in undisturbed possession of their property when Paul Kruger was alive. "The poor devils must be sorry now," he said, "that they ever sang 'God save the Queen' when the British troops came into the Transvaal, for I have seen, in the course of my duties, that a Kafir's life nowadays was not worth a ——, and I believe that no man regretted the change of flags now more than the Kafirs of Transvaal." This information was superfluous, for personal contact with the Natives of Transvaal had convinced us of the fact. They say it is only the criminal who has any reason to rejoice over the presence of the Union Jack, because in his case the cat-o'-nine-tails, except for very serious crimes, has been abolished.

"Some of the poor creatures," continued the policeman, "I knew to be fairly comfortable, if not rich, and they enjoyed the possession of their stock, living in many instances just like Dutchmen. Many of these are now being forced to leave their homes. Cycling along this road you will meet several of them in search of new homes, and if ever there was a fool's errand, it is that of a Kafir trying to find a new home for his stock and family just now."

"And what do you think, Baas Officer, must eventually be the lot of a people under such unfortunate circumstances?" we asked.

"I think," said the policeman, "that it must serve them right. They had no business to hanker after British rule, to cheat and plot with the enemies of their Republic for the overthrow of their Government. Why did they not assist the forces of their Republic during the war instead of supplying the English with scouts and intelligence? Oom Paul would not have died of a broken heart and he would still be there to protect them. Serve them right, I say."

So saying he spurred his horse, which showed a clean pair of hoofs. He left us rather abruptly, for we were about to ask why we, too, of Natal and the Cape were suffering, for we, being originally British subjects, never "cheated and plotted with the enemies of our Colonies", but he was gone and left us still cogitating by the roadside.

Proceeding on our journey we next came upon a native trek and heard the same old story of prosperity on a Dutch farm: they had raised an average 800 bags of grain each season, which, with the increase of stock and sale of wool, gave a steady income of about 150 Pounds per year after the farmer had taken his share. There were gossipy rumours about somebody having met some one who said that some one else had overheard a conversation between the Baas and somebody else, to the effect that the Kafirs were getting too rich on his property. This much involved tale incidentally conveys the idea that the Baas was himself getting too rich on his farm. For the Native provides his own seed, his own cattle, his own labour for the ploughing, the weeding and the reaping, and after bagging his grain he calls in the landlord to receive his share, which is fifty per cent of the entire crop.

All had gone well till the previous week when the Baas came to the native tenants with the story that a new law had been passed under which "all my oxen and cows must belong to him, and my family to work for 2 Pounds a month, failing which he gave me four days to leave the farm."

We passed several farm-houses along the road, where all appeared pretty tranquil as we went along, until the evening which we spent in the open country, somewhere near the boundaries of the Hoopstad and Boshof districts; here a regular circus had gathered. By a "circus" we mean the meeting of groups of families, moving to every point of the compass, and all bivouacked at this point in the open country where we were passing. It was heartrending to listen to the tales of their cruel experiences derived from the rigour of the Natives' Land Act. Some of their cattle had perished on the journey, from poverty and lack of fodder, and the native owners ran a serious risk of imprisonment for travelling with dying stock. The experience of one of these evicted tenants is typical of the rest, and illustrates the cases of several we met in other parts of the country.

Kgobadi, for instance, had received a message describing the eviction of his father-in-law in the Transvaal Province, without notice, because he had refused to place his stock, his family, and his person at the disposal of his former landlord, who now refuses to let him remain on his farm except on these conditions. The father-in-law asked that Kgobadi should try and secure a place for him in the much dreaded "Free" State as the Transvaal had suddenly become uninhabitable to Natives who cannot become servants; but "greedy folk hae lang airms", and Kgobadi himself was proceeding with his family and his belongings in a wagon, to inform his people-in-law of his own eviction, without notice, in the "Free" State, for a similar reason to that which sent his father-in-law adrift. The Baas had exacted from him the services of himself, his wife and his oxen, for wages of 30s. a month, whereas Kgobadi had been making over 100 Pounds a year, besides retaining the services of his wife and of his cattle for himself. When he refused the extortionate terms the Baas retaliated with a Dutch note, dated the 30th day of June, 1913, which ordered him to "betake himself from the farm of the undersigned, by sunset of the same day, failing which his stock would be seized and impounded, and himself handed over to the authorities for trespassing on the farm."

A drowning man catches at every straw, and so we were again and again appealed to for advice by these sorely afflicted people. To those who were not yet evicted we counselled patience and submission to the absurd terms, pending an appeal to a higher authority than the South African Parliament and finally to His Majesty the King who, we believed, would certainly disapprove of all that we saw on that day had it been brought to his notice. As for those who were already evicted, as a Bechuana we could not help thanking God that Bechuanaland (on the western boundary of this quasi-British Republic) was still entirely British. In the early days it was the base of David Livingstone's activities and peaceful mission against the

Portuguese and Arab slave trade. We suggested that they might negotiate the numerous restrictions against the transfer of cattle from the Western Transvaal and seek an asylum in Bechuanaland. We wondered what consolation we could give to these roving wanderers if the whole of Bechuanaland were under the jurisdiction of the relentless Union Parliament.

It was cold that afternoon as we cycled into the "Free" State from Transvaal, and towards evening the southern winds rose. A cutting blizzard raged during the night, and native mothers evicted from their homes shivered with their babies by their sides. When we saw on that night the teeth of the little children clattering through the cold, we thought of our own little ones in their Kimberley home of an evening after gambolling in their winter frocks with their schoolmates, and we wondered what these little mites had done that a home should suddenly become to them a thing of the past.

Kgobadi's goats had been to kid when he trekked from his farm; but the kids, which in halcyon times represented the interest on his capital, were now one by one dying as fast as they were born and left by the roadside for the jackals and vultures to feast upon.

This visitation was not confined to Kgobadi's stock, Mrs. Kgobadi carried a sick baby when the eviction took place, and she had to transfer her darling from the cottage to the jolting ox-wagon in which they left the farm. Two days out the little one began to sink as the result of privation and exposure on the road, and the night before we met them its little soul was released from its earthly bonds. The death of the child added a fresh perplexity to the stricken parents. They had no right or title to the farm lands through which they trekked: they must keep to the public roads — the only places in the country open to the outcasts if they are possessed of a travelling permit. The deceased child had to be buried, but where, when, and how?

This young wandering family decided to dig a grave under cover of the darkness of that night, when no one was looking, and in that crude manner the dead child was interred — and interred amid fear and trembling, as well as the throbs of a torturing anguish, in a stolen grave, lest the proprietor of the spot, or any of his servants, should surprise them in the act. Even criminals dropping straight from the gallows have an undisputed claim to six feet of ground on which to rest their criminal remains, but under the cruel operation of the Natives' Land Act little children, whose only crime is that God did not make them white, are sometimes denied that right in their ancestral home.

Numerous details narrated by these victims of an Act of Parliament kept us awake all that night, and by next morning we were glad enough to hear no more of the sickening procedure of extermination voluntarily instituted by the South African Parliament. We had spent a hideous night under a bitterly cold sky, conditions to which hundreds of our unfortunate countrymen and countrywomen in various parts of the country are condemned by the provisions of this Parliamentary land plague. At five o'clock in the morning the cold seemed to redouble its energies; and never before did we so fully appreciate the Master's saying: "But pray ye that your flight be not in the winter."

Chapter V Another Night with the Sufferers

> Heureux ceux qui sont morts dans le calme des soirs,
> Avant ces jours affreux de carnage et de haine!
> Ils se sont endormis, le coeur rempli d'espoirs,
> Dans un reve d'amour et de concorde humaine!

Ils n'ont pas entendu la sinistre remeur
Qui monte des hameaux consumes par la flamme,
Ni les cris des enfants et des vierges en pleurs,
Ni le gemissement des vieillards et des femmes!
Heureux les morts!
Maurice Kufferath.

We parted sadly from these unfortunate nomads of an ungrateful and inhospitable country, after advising them to trek from the Union into the arid deserts of Bechuanaland. In our advice we laid special stress upon the costliness of such an expedition as theirs and upon the many and varying regulations to be complied with, on such a trek, through the Western Transvaal. But, cost whatever it may, they, like ourselves, understood that as the law stood they would be better off and safer beyond the boundaries of the Union.

From here we worked our way into the Hoopstad district. There we saw some Natives who were, as it were, on pins and needles, their landlords having given them a few days in which to consider the advisability of either accepting the new conditions or leaving their houses. Our advice to these tenants was to accept, for the time being, any terms offered by their landlords, pending an appeal to His Majesty the King; we also passed through a few farms where the white farmers were visibly sympathetic towards the harried Natives. Some of the white farmers were accepting Natives as tenants on their farms in defiance of the law. We naturally thanked these for their humanity and went our way, promising never to disclose their magnanimity to the Government officials. "What has suddenly happened?" one of these landlords asked. "We were living so nicely with your people, and why should the law unsettle them in this manner?"

We may here mention that a fortnight later we were in General Botha's constituency in the Transvaal. A few days before we arrived there a meeting of white farmers was held at one of the Dutch farm-houses at which it was resolved to take the fullest advantage of the new law, which had placed the entire native population in the hands of the farmers. It was further resolved that a Kafir who refused to become a servant should at once be consigned to the road.

A similar resolution was passed at another meeting of landlords at another place. Part of the proceedings of this meeting was reported in some, though not all, of the Dutch newspapers. Without breaking our promise not to disclose any names of landlords who felt it a duty to resist injustice, even though it bears the garb of law, we will mention Mr. X., a Boer farmer, of the farm ——, near Thingamejig, between the town of —— and the river ——. He protested at the meeting, stating that the Transvaalers were not compelled to turn the Natives out, and that they were only debarred from taking any new native tenants; that it was wicked to expel a Kafir from the farm for no reason whatever, and so make him homeless, since he could not, if evicted, go either to another farm or back to his old place. For expressing his views so frankly Mr. X. was threatened by his compatriots with physical violence! His opponents also said that, if he continued to harbour Kafirs on his farm as tenants, they would hold him responsible for any stock that they might lose. The incidents of the meeting were related to the Natives by Mr. X. himself. He told the Natives, further, that he would go to the expense of fencing his farm with the Natives inside, so that they may be out of the reach of his infuriated neighbours.

We spent the next night in some native huts on a farm in the district of Hoopstad. On that occasion we met a man who had had a month's notice to leave his farm, and was going from farm to farm in search of a new place. He had heard alarming stories about evictions wherever he went. During that evening we were treated to some more pitiful stories concerning the atrocities of the wretched land Act. Many native wanderers had actually passed that farm during the preceding few days, trudging aimlessly from place to place in search of some farmer who might give them a shelter. At first they thought the stories about a new law were inventions or exaggerations, but their own desperate straits and the prevailing native dislocation soon taught them otherwise.

The similarity in the experiences of the sufferers would make monotonous reading if given individually, but there are instances here and there which give variety to the painful record, and these should yield the utmost satisfaction to the promoters of the Act, in proving to them the fell measure of their achievement. One example of these experiences was that of a white farmer who had induced a thrifty Native in another district to come and farm on his estate. The contract was duly executed about the end of May, 1913. It was agreed that the Native should move over to the new place after gathering his crops and sharing them with his old landlord, which he did in the third week in June. On his arrival, however, the new landlord's attitude towards him aroused his suspicions; his suspicions were confirmed when, after some hesitation, the landlord told him that their contract was illegal. Having already left his old place the legal embargo was also against his return there, and so his only course was to leave that place and wander about with his stock and family. They went in the direction of Kroonstad, and they have not been heard of since.

The next example is that of the oldest man in the "Free" State. He had been evicted (so we were told during that evening on the farm) along with his aged wife, his grey-headed children, the children's children and grandchildren. We may here add that we read a confirmation of this case in the English weekly newspaper of Harrismith. The paper's reference to this case will also illustrate the easy manner in which these outrageous evictions are reported in white newspapers. There is no reference to the sinister undercurrent and hardships attending these evictions. The paper in question, the `Harrismith Chronicle', simply says: —

== *An ancient couple*

A venerable Native whose age is no less than 119 years, accompanied by his wife, aged 98, and a son who is approaching 80, left Harrismith on Tuesday by train for Volksrust. The old man acquired some property in the Transvaal, and is leaving this district to start a new home with as much interest in the venture as if he were a stripling of twenty. The old lady had to be carried to the train, but the old man walked fairly firmly. The aged couple were the centre of much kindly attraction, and were made as comfortable as possible for their journey by the railway officials. It is difficult to realize in these days of rapid change that in the departure from the "Free" State of this venerable party we are losing from our midst a man who was born in 1794, and has lived in no less than three centuries of time. Good luck to them both; may they still live long and prosper! ==

Now, as a matter of fact, this "ancient couple" had not left the "Free" State of their own free will. Their stock had been expelled from their grazing areas, and they were told that they could only continue to graze if the centenarian tenant agreed to supply a certain number of labourers to work on the landowner's farm and with his sons ceased to do any ploughing as tenants. This system of sharing the crops has been followed ever since the Boers planted themselves in the "Free" State, and the family had had no other means of support. Happily the aid of Providence in the case of this "ancient couple" was speedy, as the old people quickly found an asylum on the farm of Mr. P. ka I. Seme, a native solicitor in the Transvaal.

At the same place on the same evening we were told of a conversation between a well-known Dutchman and a Native. "The object of this law," said the Burgher, "is to goad the Natives into rebellion, so that the Government may legally confiscate what little ground was left to them, and hand over the dispossessed Kafirs and their families to work for the farmers, just for their food." The policy of goading the Natives into rebellion is not wholly foreign to Colonial policy; but the horrible cruelty to which live stock is exposed under the new Act is altogether a new departure. King Solomon says, "The righteous man regardeth the life of his beast, but the tender mercies of the wicked are cruel"; but there is a Government of professed Bible readers who, in defiance of all Scriptural precepts, pass a law which penalizes a section of the community along with their oxen, sheep, goats, horses and donkeys on account of the colour of their owners. The penalty clause (Section 5) imposes a fine of 100 Pounds on a landowner who accommodates a Native on his farm; and if after the fine is paid the Native leaves his stock on the farm to go and look for a fresh place, there will be an additional fine of 5 Pounds for every day that the Native's cattle remain on that farm. They must take the road immediately and be kept moving day and night until they die of starvation, or until the owner (who is debarred, by Section 1, from purchasing a pasturage for his cattle) disposes of them to a white man.

Such cruelty to dumb animals is as unwarranted as it is unprecedented. It reads cruel enough on paper, but we wish that the reader had accompanied us on one journey, say, during the cold snap in the first week in August, when we travelled from Potchefstroom to Vereeniging, and seen the flocks of those evicted Natives that we met. We frequently met those roving pariahs, with their hungry cattle, and wondered if the animals were not more deserving of pity than their owners. It may be the cattle's misfortune that they have a black owner, but it is certainly not their fault, for sheep have no choice in the selection of a colour for their owners, and no cows or goats are ever asked to decide if the black boy who milks them shall be their owner, or but a herd in the employ of a white man; so why should they be starved on account of the colour of their owners? We knew of a law to prevent cruelty to animals, but had never thought that we should live to meet in one day so many dumb creatures making silent appeals to Heaven for protection against the law. "What man has nerve to do, man has not nerve to see", and oh! if those gifted Parliamentarians could have been mustered here to witness the wretched results of one of their fine days' work for a fine day's pay! But "they bind heavy burdens and grievous to be borne", then draw their Parliamentary emoluments and retire to the quiet of their comfortable homes, to enjoy more rest than is due to toilers who have served both God and humanity.

During this same night in Hoopstad district we were also told of the visit of a Dutch farmer in the middle of June, 1913, to his native tenants. One of the Natives — named Kgabale — was rather old. His two sons are delving in the gold mines of Johannesburg, and return home each spring time to help the old man and their two young sisters to do the ploughing. The daughters tend the fields and Kgabale looks after the stock. By this means they have been enabled to lead a respectable life and to pay the landowner fifty per cent. of the produce every year, besides the taxes levied by the Government on Natives. Three weeks before our visit, the farmer came to cancel Kgabale's verbal contract with him and to turn the family into unpaid servants, in return for the privilege of squatting on his farm. As Kgabale himself was too old to work, the farmer demanded of him that his two sons should return immediately from Johannesburg to render manual service on his farm, failing which, the old man should forthwith betake himself from the place. He gave Kgabale seven days to deliver his two sons.

Naturally this decision came upon Kgabale and his daughters like a bolt from the blue. The poor old man wandered from place to place, trying to find some one — and it took him two days to do so — who could write, so as to dictate a letter to his sons in Johannesburg, informing them of what had happened. The week expired before he could get a reply from Johannesburg. The landlord, in a very abusive mood, again demanded the instant arrival of his two sons from Johannesburg, to commence work at the farm-house the very next morning. Kgabale spent the whole night praying that at least one of his sons might come. By daybreak next morning no answer had arrived, and the Dutchman came and set fire to the old man's houses, and ordered him then and there to quit the farm. It was a sad sight to see the feeble old man, his aged wife and his daughters driven in this way from a place which they had regarded as their home. In the ordinary course, such a calamity could have been made more tolerable by moving to the next farm and there await the arrival and advice of his sons; but now, under the Natives' Land Act, no sympathetic landowner would be permitted to shelter them for a single day. So Kgabale was said to have gone in the direction of Klerksdorp.

One of the sons arrived a week after the catastrophe. He found his old home in ruins, and that his aged parents and their children had become victims of the turpitude of an Act of Parliament. The son went in search of his relatives across the Vaal, but it was not known if they succeeded in finding the refuge which the law had made unlawful.

Among the squatters on the same farm as Kgabale was a widow named Maria. Her husband in his lifetime had lived as a tenant on the farm, ploughing in shares until his death. After his death Maria kept on the contract and made a fair living. Her son and daughter, aged fourteen and sixteen respectively, took turns at herding her cattle and assisting the mother in other ways. During the ploughing season, they hired assistance to till the fields, but they themselves tended and reaped the harvest and delivered 50 per cent of the produce to the landowner. Such were the conditions on which she was allowed to live on the farm. Maria, being a widow, and her son being but a youth, it was hoped that the landlord would propose reasonable terms for her; but instead, his proposal was that she should dispose of her stock and indenture her children to him. This sinister proposal makes it evident that farmers not only expect Natives to render them free labour, but they actually wish the Natives to breed slaves for them. Maria found it difficult to comply with her landlord's demand, and as she had no husband, from whom labour could be exacted, the Dutchman ordered her to "clear out, and," he added with an oath, "you must get another man before you reach your next place of abode, as the law will not permit you to stay there till you have a man to work for the Baas." Having given this counsel the landlord is said to have set fire to Maria's thatched cottage, and as the chilly south-easter blew the smoke of her burning home towards the north-west, Maria, with her bedclothes on her head, and on the heads of her son and daughter, and carrying her three-year-old boy tied to her back, walked off from the farm, driving her cows before her. In parting from the endeared associations of their late home, for one blank and unknown, the children were weeping bitterly. Nor has any news of the fate of this family been received since they were forced out on this perilous adventure.

Chapter VI Our Indebtedness to White Women

O woman! in our hours of ease
Uncertain, coy, and hard to please,
And variable as the shade
By the light quivering aspen made;
When pain and anguish wring the brow,
A ministering angel thou.
Scott.

Some farmers (unfortunately too few) who had at first intended to change the status of their native tenants, had been obliged to abandon the idea owing to the determined opposition of their wives. One such case was particularly interesting. Thus, at Dashfontein, the wife of a Dutch farmer, a Mr. V., on whose property some native families were squatting, got up, one morning, and found the kitchen-maid very disagreeable. The morning coffee had been made right enough, but the maid's "Morre, Nooi" (Good morning, ma'am) was rather sullen and almost bordering on insolence. She did her scullery work as usual, but did not seem to care, that morning, about wasting time inquiring how baby slept, and if Nonnie had got rid of her neuralgia, and so on. She spoke only when spoken to and answered mainly in monosyllables. Mrs. V. was perplexed.

"What is the matter, Anna?" she asked.

"Nothing, Nooi," replied Anna curtly.

Mrs. V. tried some of her witty jokes, but they seemed to be wasted on Anna. After jesting with the servant had failed, scolding was next tried, but nothing seemed to bring back the girl's usual cheerfulness. "Oh, Anna," said the mistress at length, "you make me think of the olden days, when such disagreeable whims on the part of frowning maids used to be cured by ——"

Anna was evidently not listening, and, if she had heard the mistress, she did not care two straws (or one straw for that matter) what cures Mrs. V.'s great-grandmother had prescribed for sullen servant girls. In fact, Anna had become a wild Kafir, for though she went about her work in silence, her face bore an expression which seemed to speak louder than her mouth could have done. She was clearly engaged in serious thought. The mistress tried to dismiss from her mind the inexplicable attitude of her servant, but the frowning look on Anna's face made the attempts unsuccessful. The fact that when Anna went home, the previous night, she was happiness personified, did not decrease Mrs. V.'s perplexity.

"There must be something wrong," Mrs. V. concluded, after vainly trying ruse after ruse to get a smile out of her servant girl. "Something is amiss. I wonder if one of those well-dressed Kafirs from Potchefstroom had been prowling about the farm and instilling in Anna's simple mind all kinds of silly notions, about town flirts and black dandies, silk dresses in Potchefstroom and similar vuilgoed (rubbish). And if a town Kafir is going to marry Anna, where on earth am I going to get a reliable servant to whom I could securely entrust my home when I have occasion to go to town or to the seaside on a shorter or longer vacation? Who could cook and attend to my husband's and children's peculiar wants, if Anna is going to leave us? It seems certain that Anna's heart is not on the farm," she said to herself. "It was there right enough when she went home last night, but it is clear that some one has stolen it during the night. Anna is helplessly lovesick. I must find out who it is. The swain must be found and induced to come and join, or supervise, our squatters. We cannot let him take her away, for what will the homestead be without Anna? I was looking forward to her marrying on the farm and giving her a superior cottage so that other Kafir girls may see how profitable it is to be good. Anna leaving the farm, O, nee wat! (Oh, no). We must find out who it is; but wait, there is old Gert (her father) coming, with old Jan (her uncle). I must find out from them who had been intruding into the company of their daughters last night. I should warn them to be on the alert lest Anna elopes to Potchefstroom with somebody, probably to take the train and go farther — to Johannesburg or Kimberley, as did Klein Mietje, whom I had hoped to train as our housemaid ——"

"Good morning, Auta Gert, how is Mietje and the kleintjes (little ones)?"

Auta Gert's demeanour was a greater puzzle to Mrs. V. than his daughter's when he replied, "So, so."

Mrs. V. (between horns of the same dilemma): "And you, Auta Jan?"

"Ja, Missus," replied Jan.

Mrs. V.'s perplexity was intense, for it became evident that the two Natives were there as a deputation, charged with some grave mission. Before she uttered another word the two Natives asked for an interview.

"Not to waste much time, Missus," began old Gert, "a thunderbolt has burst on the native settlement on the farm, and Dashfontein is no longer a home to us ——"

"No longer a home!" exclaimed Mrs. V. "I hope you idiotic Kafirs are not going to be so foolhardy as to leave me, leave the Baas, and leave the farm upon which your fathers and mothers lie buried. Do not you know that during this very week numbers of Natives have been calling on the Baas, asking him for places of abode, complaining that they have been turned adrift, with their little ones and their hungry animals, for refusing to become servants to farmers on whose property they had been ploughing on shares? White men have suddenly become brutes and have expelled Natives with whom they have lived from childhood — Natives whose labour made the white man wealthy are turned away by people who should treat them with gratitude. And are you going to leave your old home just when the Devil appears to have possessed himself of the hearts of most farmers? In your own interest, apart from my own and the Baas's, Auta Gert, you should have left us long ago when you could find a place elsewhere. Are you so deaf and blind as not to hear and see the change which has come over the country of late? White men formerly punished a Kafir who had done some wrong, now they worry him from sheer cussedness. You must be mad, Auta Gert, to try and leave us. What is going to become of your family and your beautiful cattle. No wonder that Anna is so upset. I have been thinking that some rondlooper (vagabond) from the towns had been trying to take her away."

As Mrs. V. spoke she was agreeably surprised to find the sobering effect which her rebuke seemed to have upon her husband's native tenants. She knew her influence over them, especially over the old native families, but in all her dealings and close association with them she could not remember an impromptu speech of hers that produced such immediate results. The faces of the two Natives brightened up, and they kept looking at one another as she spoke. At length she turned round towards the stoep and there was Anna, for the first time that morning, interested in and delighted by what she said. Usually it would have been a serious breach of the rules of the house for Anna to listen when the Missus was speaking about something that did not immediately concern her scullery duties; but Mrs. V.'s satisfaction was unbounded on seeing the bright look on her servant's face, which she had hitherto vainly sought.

"Now, you see," said Anna to her father, "I told you it would never happen if the Missus can help it."

At this, the men could scarcely suppress a laugh. The Missus looked round again, and said:

"Anna, have you Kafirs plotted to fool me this morning? Because I take such a deep interest in your welfare, you have so far forgotten yourselves that you connived with your parents to come over to my house and fool me on my own farm? What is the meaning of all this?"

Auta Gert unfolded his story. The Baas was at the native settlement the previous day. He called a meeting of the native peasants and told them of the new law, under which no Kafir can buy a farm or hire a farm. He added that, according to this law, their former relations of landlord and tenants have been made a criminal offence, for which they could be fined a hundred pounds, and he gave them ten days to decide whether they would become his servants or leave the farm.

"Go away, Auta Gert; you were dreaming, my husband would never talk such nonsense. You have been with him from childhood, long before I ever knew him, and yet you do not know that my husband is incapable of uttering anything half so wicked?"

"He said it was the law, the new law."

"Of course you need some stringent measures against the useless, sneaking and prowling loafers, but there is no fear that such laws could apply to Natives like you and Mietje and your children."

"But, Nooi, the Baas told us to leave the farm as the law did not permit him to ——"

"Get you gone, Auta Gert, he was joking. You must know that the law did not buy this farm. The old Baas purchased it from Baas Philander. I personally helped to add up the number of morgen and to calculate the money, and there was not a penny piece from any Government. Go home, Auta Gert, and leave everything to me, and do not let me hear you saying Dashfontein is no longer your home."

"Well, Nooi," assented the Natives with some relief, "if you say it is all right, then it must be so, and we will go back and reap our mealies in peace, and if a policeman comes round demanding a hundred pounds we will tell him to arrest us and take us to the Nooi of the farm. Good-bye, Nooi."

"Good-bye, Auta Gert; good-bye, Auta Jan —— Poor Anna, my dear little maid, why did you not tell Nooi this morning that you were worried over this matter. Really, Anna, I was thinking that you were lovesick. How did poor old Mietje take it? Sadly, did she. Well, I will speak to the Baas about it. He had no business to attempt to bring bad luck over us by disturbing our peaceful Natives with such godless tidings. Tell your mother that Nooi says it will be all right."

A few days later, Hendrik Prins, the farm manager in the employ of Mr. V., was due at the native settlement to see the steam sheller at work and also to receive the landowner's share of the produce. Instead of Prins, Mr. V. attended in person. Each Native regarded this unusual occurrence as the signal for their impending eviction and thought that day would see their last transaction with their old master and landlord.

Mr. V. counted the separate bags filled with mealies and Kafir corn placed in groups around the sheller. He counted no fewer than 12,300 bags, and knew that his share would total 6,150, representing about 3,000 Pounds gross. Could he ever succeed in getting so much, with so little trouble, if poor whites tilled his lands instead of these Natives? he thought. After all, his dear Johanna was right. This law is blind and must be resisted. It gives more consideration to the so-called poor whites (a respectable term for lazy whites), than to the owners of the ground. He, there and then, resolved to resist it and take the consequences.

The grain was all threshed; a number of native girls were busy sewing up the bags, and the engine-driver ordered his men to yoke his oxen and pull the machine away. Mr. V. ordered Auta Gert to call all the `volk' together as he had something to tell them. Auta Gert, knowing the determination of his mistress, did so in confidence that they were about to receive some glad tidings. But the other folks came forward with a grievous sense of wrong. The fact that some Natives on the adjoining property had been turned away three days before and sent homeless about the country, their places being taken by others, who, tired of roaming about and losing nearly everything, had come in as serfs did not allay their fears. Auta Hans was already conjuring up visions of a Johannesburg speculator literally "taking" his Cape shorthorns for a mere bagatelle, as they did to William Ranco, another evicted squatter from Hoopstad.

Mr. V., the farmer, mounted a handy wagon hard by and commenced to address the crowd of blacks who gathered around the wagon at the call of Gert.

"Attention! Listen," he said. "You will remember that I was here last month and explained to you the new law. Well, I understand that that explanation created the greatest amount of unrest amongst the Natives in the huts on my farm. Personally, I am very sorry that it ever came to that, but let me tell you that your Nooi, my wife, says it is not right that the terms under which we have lived in the past should be disturbed. I agree with her that it is unjust, and that the good Lord, who has always blessed us, will turn His face from us if people are unsettled and sent away from the farm in a discontented mood." (Loud and continued applause, during which Mr. V. took out his pouch of Magaliesburg tobacco and lit his pipe.) "The Nooi," he continued after a few puffs, "says we must not obey this law: she even says, if it comes to physical ejectment, or if they take me to prison, she is prepared to go to Pretoria in person and interview General Botha." (More cheers, during which the Natives dispersed to cart away their mealies amidst general satisfaction.)

* * * * *

The writer visited Dashfontein in July, 1913, when the above narrative was given him word for word by old Gert.

As old Gert narrated the story, Aunt Mietje, his wife, who had had timely notice of the impending visit of the morulaganyi (editor) from her husband (who slaughtered a sheep in honour of the occasion), superintended with interesting expectations over frizzling items in the frying-pan on her fireplace. Her bright eyes, beaming from under her headkerchief, suggested how she must have been the undisputed belle of her day. The rough wooden table was covered with the best linen in the native settlement, and on it were laid some clean plates, and the old yet shining cutlery reserved for special occasions, besides other signs of an approaching evening meal. Having learnt the art from an experienced housewife on whose farm her people were squatting, and improved upon her teaching, she was famous in the neighbourhood for the excellence of her cooking. Her only worry in that department was her seeming lack of success in training her daughters up to her elevation. She is usually sent for when important visitors come to Dashfontein, and would then don her best costume of coloured German print, and carry down with her the spotless apron which Mrs. V. gave her the preceding New Year; and in spite of her advancing years, she would cause Anna, and every other upstart at the homestead, instinctively to play second fiddle to her. And when we suggested that our wife could measure swords (or, shall we say, forks) with her as a cook, she giggled and remembered some white man's proverb about the proof of the pudding being in the eating.

After the harrowing experience of the previous week, during which we were forced to see our fellow-beings hounded out of their homes, and the homes broken up; their lifelong earnings frittered away by a law of the land, their only crime being the atrocious one of having the same colour of skin as our own, and finding ourselves suddenly landed on an oasis, the farm of a kind Dutchman and his noble wife, on whose property, and by whose leave, little black piccaninnies still played about in spite of the law, it can be readily understood with what comfort we sat down and did justice to the good things provided by Aunt Mietje. In the course of her preparation every step of hers suggested that she entertained no sort of misprised opinion about her superiority over her compeers; and nothing pleased her better than when she dazzled her husband and family connexions with deeds which proved her superiority over her contemporaries, in everything that tends to make the virtuous and industrious house-wife. She gave a dramatic ending to her husband's narrative when she said —

"Who would have thought that Hannetje, naughty little Hannetje, who was so troublesome when my sister used to nurse her — who would have thought that she would ever prove to be the salvation of our people? Who ever anticipated that all the strong Boers, on whom we had relied, would desert us when the fate of our whole tribe hung in the balance? Natives have been moving from north to south, and from south to north, all searching at the same time for homes and grazing for their cattle. During the last few weeks the roads were hidden in clouds of dust, sent up by hundreds of hoofs of hundreds of cattle, their owners with them, vainly seeking places of refuge; but in the case of Dashfontein, we reclined on a veritable Mount Ararat, by grace of naughty little Hannetje, whom God in His mysterious foresight had raised up to be Mrs. van V., proprietress of Dashfontein. If my prayers are of any value, God will appoint in heaven a special place for her when she gets there, though, for the sake of our people, I hope that time is very far distant. However, I hope to be somewhere near: in truth, I should like to accompany her, when Elijah's chariot comes for her soul, so as to render her what little aid I can on board, when she soars through unknown tracts of space to the spirit world on high, so that if there be any uncomfortable questions about her maiden vagaries, I may be there to attest that she has since atoned a hundred fold for each, and thus accelerate her promotion. No no, Hannetje is not a Boer vrouw, she is an angel."

Chapter VII Persecution of Coloured Women in the Orange Free State

Ripe persecution, like the plant
Whose nascence Mocha boasted,
Some bitter fruit produced, whose worth
Was never known till roasted.

When the Free State ex-Republicans made use of the South African Constitution — a Constitution which Lord Gladstone says is one after the Boer sentiment — to ruin the coloured population, they should at least have confined their persecution to the male portion of the blacks (as is done in a milder manner in the other three Provinces), and have left the women and children alone. According to this class legislation, no native woman in the Province of the Orange "Free" State can reside within a municipality (whether with or without her parents, or her husband) unless she can produce a permit showing that she is a servant in the employ of a white person, this permit being signed by the Town Clerk. All repressive measures under the old Republic (which, in matters of this kind, always showed a regard for the suzerainty of Great Britain) were mildly applied. Now, under the Union, the Republicans are told by the Imperial authorities that since they are self-governing they have the utmost freedom of action, including freedom to do wrong, without any fear of Imperial interference. Of this licence the white inhabitants of the Union are making the fullest use. Like a mastiff long held in the leash they are urging the application of all the former stringent measures enacted against the blacks, and the authorities, in obedience to their electoral supporters, are enforcing these measures with the utmost rigour against the blacks because they have no votes.

Hence, whereas the pass regulations were formerly never enforced by the Boers against clergymen's wives or against the families of respectable native inhabitants, now a minister's wife has not only to produce a pass on demand, but, like every woman of colour, she has to pay a shilling for a fresh pass at the end of the month, so that a family consisting of, say, a mother and five daughters pay the municipality 6s. every month, whether as a penalty for the colour of their skins or a penalty for their sex it is not clear which.

There is some unexplained anomaly in this woman's pass business. If the writer were to go and live in the "Free" State, he could apply for and obtain letters of exemption from the ordinary pass laws; but if his wife, who has had a better schooling and enjoyed an older civilization than he, were to go and reside in the "Free" State with her daughters, all of them would be forced to carry passes on their persons, and be called upon to ransack their skirt pockets at any time in the public streets at the behest of male policemen in quest of their passes. Several white men are at present undergoing long terms of imprisonment inflicted by the Orange "Free" State Circuit Courts for criminally outraging coloured women whom the pass laws had placed in the hollow of the hands of these ruffians. Still many more mothers are smothering evidence of similar outrages upon innocent daughters — cases that could never have happened under ordinary circumstances.

The Natives of the "Free" State have made all possible constitutional appeals against these outrages. In reply to their petitions the Provincial Government blames the municipalities. The latter blame the law and the Union Parliament, and there the matter ends. We have read the "Free" State law which empowers the municipalities to frame regulations for the control of Natives, *etc.*, but it must be confessed that our limited intelligence could discern nothing in it which could be construed as imposing any dire penalties on municipalities which emancipate their coloured women from the burden of the insidious pass law and tax. Hon. Mr. H. Burton, as already stated, was Minister for Native Affairs before the Union Government surrendered to the "Free" State reactionaries. A deputation consisting of Mrs. A. S. Gabashane, Mrs. Kotsi and Mrs. Louw, women from Bloemfontein — the first-named being a clergyman's wife — waited on him in Capetown on the subject of these grievances, and he assured them that in response to representations made by the Native Congress, he had already written to Dr. Ramsbottom, the Provincial Administrator, asking him to persuade the "Free" State municipalities to relieve the native women from this burden. And if to relieve native women in the "Free" State from a burden which obtains nowhere else in the Union were unlawful, as the municipalities aver, Mr. Burton — a K.C. — would have been the last person to ask them to break the law.

Subsequently the women petitioned Lady Gladstone for her intercession. But we wonder if the petition was ever handed to Lady Gladstone by the responsible authority who, in this instance, would have been the Department of Native Affairs. Notwithstanding all these efforts, native women in the "Free" State are still forced to buy passes every month or go to prison, and they are still exposed to the indecent provision of the law authorizing male constables to insult them by day and by night, without distinction.

After exhausting all these constitutional means on behalf of their women, and witnessing the spread of the trouble to the women and children of the country districts under the Natives' Land Act, the male Natives of the municipalities of the Province of the Orange "Free" State saw their women folk throwing off their shawls and taking the "law" into their own hands. A crowd of 600 women, in July, 1913, marched to the Municipal Offices at Bloemfontein and asked to see the Mayor. He was not in, so they called for the Town Clerk. The Deputy-Mayor came out, and they deposited before him a bag containing their passes of the previous month and politely signified their intention not to buy any more passes. Then there occurred what `John Bull' would call, "——l with the lid off".

At Jagersfontein there was a similar demonstration, led by a jet-black Mozambique lady. She and a number of others were arrested and sentenced to various terms of imprisonment. The sentences ranged from about three weeks to three months, and the fines from 10s. to 3 Pounds. They all refused to pay the fines, and said their little ones could be entrusted to the care of Providence till their mothers and sisters have broken the shackles of oppression by means of passive resistance. As the prison authorities were scarcely prepared for such a sudden influx of prisoners there was not sufficient accommodation for fifty-two women, who were conveyed on donkey carts to the adjoining village of Fauresmith.

When this happened, Winburg, the old capital of the "Free" State, also had a similar trouble. Eight hundred women marched from the native location to the Town Hall, singing hymns, and addressed the authorities. They were tired of making friendly appeals which bore no fruit from year's end to year's end, so they had resolved, they said, to carry no more passes, much less to pay a shilling each per month, *per capita*, for passes. A procession of so many women would attract attention even in Piccadilly, but in a "Free" State dorp it was a stupendous event, and it made a striking impression. The result was that many of the women were arrested and sent to prison, but they all resolutely refused to pay their fines, and there was a rumour that the Central Government had been appealed to for funds and for material to fit out a new jail to cope with the difficulty.

This movement served to exasperate the authorities, who rigorously enforced the law and sent them to jail. The first batch of prisoners from Bloemfontein were conveyed south to Edenburg; and as further batches came down from Bloemfontein they had to be retransferred north to Kroonstad. In the course of our tour in connexion with the Natives' Land Act in August, 1913, we spent a week-end with the Rev. A. P. Pitso, of the last-named town. Thirty-four of the women passive resisters were still incarcerated there, doing hard labour. Mrs. Pitso and Mrs. Michael Petrus went with us on the Sunday morning to visit the prisoners at the jail.

A severe shock burst upon us, inside the prison walls, when the matron withdrew the barriers and the emaciated figures of ladies and young girls of our acquaintance filed out and greeted us. It was an exceptionally cold week, and our hearts bled to see young women of Bloemfontein, who had spent all their lives in the capital and never knew what it was to walk without socks, walking the chilly cemented floors and the cold and sharp pebbles without boots. Their own boots and shoes had been taken off, they told us, and they were, throughout the winter, forced to perform hard labour barefooted.

Was ever inhumanity more cold-blooded?

Do these "Free" Staters consider their brutality less brutal
because it happens to be sanctioned by law?

Is Heaven so entirely unmindful of our case that it looks on with indifference when indignity upon indignity is heaped, not only upon our innocent men, but even upon our inoffensive women?

Tears rolled down our cheeks as we saw the cracks on their bare feet, the swellings and chronic chilblains, which made them look like sheep suffering from foot-and-mouth disease. It was torture to us to learn the kind of punishment to which they were subjected and the nature of the work they were called upon to perform; these facts were stated to us in the presence of the prison officials, and they were communicated by us to the Native Affairs Department merely as a matter of course. But what must be the effect of this brutal punishment upon girls who knew only city life? To our surprise, however, they vowed never to buy passes, even if they had to come back.

A month later, when we visited Bloemfontein, a majority of those who were at the Kroonstad jail had already returned to their homes, and the family doctors were doing a roaring trade. Their practice, too, was most likely to continue to boom as the sufferers were still determined to buy no more women's passes.

This determination caused a white man to suggest that "instead of being sent to prison with hard labour, these madcaps should be flogged" — and this because the women refuse to be outraged by law.

Our visit to Kroonstad took place just after the Circuit Court had convicted the white superintendent of the Kroonstad Native Location for an outrage upon a coloured woman. He arrested her in the location ostensibly because she could not produce her residential pass, and in the field between the location and the town through which he had to escort her to prison he perpetrated the atrocity. In sentencing him to four years' hard labour, the Chief Justice said for a similar crime upon a white woman a black man would be liable to the death penalty.

When General Botha assumed the portfolio of Native Affairs at the time of this trouble, the writer, as General Secretary of the Congress, telegraphed to him the greetings of the South African Native Congress, and pointed out to him that over two hundred coloured women were at that time languishing in jail for resenting a crime committed upon them, a crime which would have been considered serious in any other place outside the "Free" State. The chivalrous General replied in a Dutch telegram containing this very courteous reply: "It shall be my endeavour, as hitherto, to safeguard the just interests of the inhabitants of this land irrespective of colour."

General Botha's assurances are so sweet, especially when they are made to persons who are not in a position to influence his electoral support. The Natives, who know the "sweets" of these assurances cannot be blamed if they analyse the Premier's assurances in the light of their past experience, especially the phrase "as hitherto". To them it conveys but one idea, namely, "If the future policy of the South African Government found it convenient to send coloured women to prison in order to please the ruling whites, they will, *as hitherto*, not hesitate to do so."

While on the subject of native women, it is deeply to be regretted that during this year, while the Empire is waging a terrible war for the cause of liberty, His Excellency the Governor-General in South Africa should have seen his way to issue a Basutoland Proclamation — No. 3 of 1915. This law decrees that under certain penalties, no native woman will be permitted to leave Basutoland "without the permission of her husband or guardian". The Proclamation on the face of it may look comparatively harmless, but its operation will have wide and painful ramifications amounting to no less than an entrenchment of the evils embraced in polygamy; and in carrying out this decree civilization will have to join hands with barbarism to perpetuate the bondage, and accentuate the degradation, of Basuto women.

It is a fact that no respectable Mosuto woman wants to leave her husband or guardian; but the economic conditions of to-day press very heavily on polygamous wives. Their lord and master finding himself no longer able to provide for half a dozen houses at a time, bestows on them the burden and anxieties of wifehood without its joys, namely, a husband's undivided care and the comforts due to wives in monogamous marriages.

Some of these polygamous wives have from time to time sought relief in emigrating to European centres where they could earn their own living and send food and raiment to their little ones. A woman cannot always be blamed for having entered into a polygamous marriage. More often than not, she did so in obedience to the wishes of her aged parents. The old people, in many instances, have judged present day economics from the standard of their own happy days when there was plenty of land and rainfalls were more regular; when the several wives and children of a rich cattle-owner could always have enough grain, eat meat, drink milk and live happily. But times are altered and even a monogamist finds the requirements of one wife quite a stupendous handful. The country is so congested that the little arable land left them yields hardly any produce. I have seen it suggested in official documents that sheep-breeding should be limited in Basutoland as there is not enough grazing for the flocks. And under this economic stress these surplus wives are sometimes driven to accept the overtures of unscrupulous men who gradually induce them to wallow in sin; hence too, they give birth to an inferior type of Basuto.

That such a law should be adopted during the reign of Chief Griffith, their first Christian Chief and the first monogamist who ever ruled the Basuto, is disappointing. And while we resent the policy of the British authorities in the Union, who promote the interests of the whites by repressing the blacks, we shall likewise object to an attempt on the part of the same authorities in the native territories to protect the comfort of black men by degrading black women. God knows that the lot of the black woman in South Africa is bad as it is. One has but to read the report of the Commission recently appointed by the Union Government to inquire into cases of assault on women to find that their condition is getting worse. Presumably the evidence was too bad for publication, but the report would seem to show that in South Africa, a country where prostitution was formerly unknown, coloured women are gradually perverted and demoralized into a cesspool for the impurities of the family lives of all the nationalities in the sub-continent.

In her primitive state, the native girl was protected against seduction and moral ruin by drastic penalties against the seducer, which safeguards have since the introduction of civilized rule been done away with. With tribes just groping their way from barbarism towards civilization natural hygienic and moral laws have been trampled upon, and for this state of affairs the white man's rule is not wholly free from blame. It should be a crime to defile a potential mother and a woman should continue to be regarded as the cradle of the race and her person remain sacred and inviolate under the law, as was the case in former times.

The only charge that could be brought up against primitive native socialism was that by tolerating polygamy it had incidentally legalized concubinage; but taking all circumstances into consideration, it is doubtful if the systematic prostitution of to-day is a happy substitution for the polygamy of the past.

There were no mothers of unwanted babies; no orphanages, because there were no stray children; the absence of extreme wealth and dire poverty prevented destitution, and the Natives had little or no insanity; they had no cancer or syphilis, and no venereal diseases because they had no prostitutes.

Have we not a right to expect a better state of affairs under civilized European rule?

It is apparently in revolt of similar horrible conditions that when the war broke out, British and Continental women were fighting for the vote with a view to liberating their sex and race from kindred impurities, for the soul rises up in "divine discontent" against a state of affairs which no nation should tolerate — evils to which the coloured women of South Africa are now a prey.

To this kind of degeneracy may also be traced the undoing of the finer elements of the native social system, the undermining of their health and of the erstwhile splendid physique of the African race and the increasing loss of the stamina of our proverbially magnificent men and women. The effect of these evils and of the abuses inherent to the liquor traffic is manifest in several of the tribes who are to-day but shadows of their former selves.

The safeguarding of our maidens and women folk from the evils of drink, greed and outrages resulting from indefensible pass laws and the elimination of bad habits among men by a rightful policy will restore that efficiency, loyalty, and contentment which aforetime were the boast of pioneer administrators in British South Africa, and which if fostered will render them a magnificent asset to the Empire for all time.

But as often as the coloured woman has been attacked she has humbly presented "the other cheek". Evidence of her characteristic humility is to be found in the action of the coloured women of the "Free" State, whose persecution by the South African Government, at the instance of certain "Free" State Municipalities, prompted the writing of this chapter. After the war broke out (the Bloemfontein `Friend' tells us) the native women of that city forgot their own difficulties, joined sewing classes, and helped to send clothing to the afflicted Belgians in Europe. Surely such useful members of the community deserve the sympathy of every right-minded person who has a voice in the conduct of British Colonial administration; so let us hope that this humble appeal on their behalf will not be in vain.

Chapter VIII At Thaba Ncho: A Secretarial Fiasco

Man's inhumanity to man makes countless thousands mourn.
Burns.

The beginning of September, 1913, found us in the Lady Brand district. Besides numerous other sufferers of the land plague, the writer was here informed of one case that was particularly distressing, of a native couple evicted from a farm in the adjoining district. After making a fruitless search for a new place of abode, they took out a travelling pass to go to Basutoland with their stock. But they never, so the story went, reached their destination. We were told that they were ambushed by some Dutchmen, who shot them down and appropriated their stock. To a stranger the news would have been incredible, but, being a Free Stater born, it sounded to us uncommonly like the occurrences that our parents said they used to witness in the early days of that precious dependency. We were further told that one of the Dutch murderers had been arrested and was awaiting his trial at the next criminal sessions. As both the native man and woman were shot, it seemed difficult to conceive how the prosecution could find the necessary evidence to sustain a charge of murder.

The trial duly came off at Bloemfontein a month or two later, and the evidence in court seemed more direct and less circumstantial than we had expected. For, not only were the stolen cattle found in the possession of the prisoner, but the bullet picked up near the bodies of the dead refugees (according to the evidence given in court) fitted the prisoner's pistol. General Hertzog personally attended the court at Bloemfontein and conducted the defence; and, presumably more by his eloquence than anything else, he convinced a white jury of the guiltlessness of the accused, who was acquitted and acclaimed outside the court by his friends as a hero. In justice to the police it must be added that they re-arrested this man and charged him with the theft, or with being in possession of the deceased Natives' cattle. On this charge the prisoner was convicted before the Circuit Court a few months later, and in sentencing him to three years, with hard labour, the presiding judge is said to have made some references to the previous trial and the manner in which the prisoner had escaped the capital sentence.

From Lady Brand we travelled south towards Wepener, not far from the Basuto frontier. Evictions around here were numerous, but beyond the inevitable hardships of families suddenly driven from home, they had not suffered any great amount of damage. Being near to the Basuto border, a Native in these parts, when ejected, can quickly take his stock across the boundary, and leaving them in friendly pastures, under sympathetic laws, go away to look for a new place. But it became abundantly clear that the influx of outsiders into Basutoland could not continue at the rate it was then proceeding without seriously complicating the land question in Basutoland, where chieftains are constantly quarrelling over small patches of arable land.

A pitiable spectacle, however, was the sight of those who had been evicted from the centre of the Orange "Free" State. It was heartrending to hear them relate the circumstances of their expulsions, and how they had spent the winter months roaming from farm to farm with their famishing stock, applying in vain for a resting place. Some farmers were apparently sympathetic, but debarred from entertaining such applications by the sword of Damocles — the 100 Pound fine in Section 5 of the Natives' Land Act — they had perforce to refuse the applicants. The farms hereabout are owned by Boers and English settlers, but many are owned by Germans, Jews, Russians, and other Continentals. Some of the proprietors do not reside on the farms at all; they are either Hebrew merchants or lawyers, living in the towns and villages away from the farms. Many have no wish to part with the Natives, who seem invariably to have treated their landlords well, but they are forced to do so by the law.

It seems a curious commentary on the irony of things that South Africa, which so tyrannically chases her own Natives from the country, receives at this very time with open arms Polish, Finnish, Russian and German Jews, who themselves are said to have fled from the tyranny of their own Governments in Europe. With a vengeance, it looks like "robbing Peter to pay Paul".

Standing by the side of a kopje, very early on that September morning, it was a relief to see the majestic tops of the mountains of Basutoland, silhouetted against the rising sun, beyond the Caledon River, which separates the "Free" State from Basutoland.

A number of fugitives were at that time driving little lots of stock across the broad and level flats which extend in the direction of the Basutoland Protectorate. How comforting to know that once they crossed the river, these exiles could rest their tired limbs and water their animals without breaking any law. Really until we saw those emaciated animals, it had never so forcibly occurred to us that it is as bad to be a black man's animal as it is to be a black man in South Africa.

To think that this "Free" State land from which these people are now expelled was at one time, and should still be, part and parcel of Basutoland; and to remember that the fathers of these Natives, who are now fleeing from the "Free" State laws, were allies of the Boers, whom they assisted to drive the Basutos from this habitable and arable part of their land; that with their own rations, their own horses, their own rifles, and often their own ammunition, they helped the Boers to force the Basutos back into their present mountain recesses, and compelled them to build fresh homes in all but uninhabitable mountain fastnesses, in many instances inaccessible to vehicles of any kind, in order (as was said at the time) to give themselves "more elbow-room"; to see them to-day fleeing from the laws of their perfidious Dutch allies, expelled from the country for which they bled and for which their fathers died; and to find that, at the risk of intensifying their own domestic problems in their now diminutive and overcrowded Mountain State, the Basutos are nobly offering an asylum to those who had helped to deprive them of their country; and to remember that this mean breach of faith, on the part of ex-Republicans towards their native allies, is facilitated by the protection of the Union Jack, sheds, in regard to the Basutos, a glorious ray of light upon black human nature.

Look at these exiles swarming towards the Basuto border, some of them with their belongings on their heads, driving their emaciated flocks attenuated by starvation and the cold. The faces of some of the children, too, are livid from the cold. It looks as if these people were so many fugitives escaping from a war, with the enemy pressing hard at their heels.

It was a distressing sight. We had never seen the likes of it since the outbreak of the Boer War, near the Transvaal border, immediately before the siege of Mafeking. Even that flight of 1899 had a buoyancy of its own, for the Boer War, unlike the present stealthy war of extermination (the law which caused this flight), was preceded by an ultimatum. But the sight of a people who had loyally paid taxation put to flight in these halcyon times, by a Parliament the huge salaries of whose members these very exiles, although unrepresented in its body, have meekly helped to pay, turned one's weeping eyes to Heaven, for, as Jean Paul says, "There above is everything he can wish for here below." But if the Native of other days has been sold by the perfidy of his Dutch allies of the day, the British soldiers and British taxpayer of the present day have been deceived by "we don't know who". They fought and died and paid to unfurl the banner of freedom in this part of the globe, and the spectacle before us is the result. This must be what A. H. Keene referred to when he said, "The British public were also dumb, and with that infinite capacity for being gulled which is so remarkable in a people proud of their common sense, acquiesced in everything."

Visiting the farms, we found some native tenants under notice to leave. We informed them that Mr. Edward Dower, the Secretary for Native Affairs, would be in Thaba Ncho the following week, and advised them to proceed to the town and lay their difficulties before this high representative of the Union Government, with a request for the use of his good offices to procure for them the Governor-General's permission to live on farms, a course provided in Section 1 of the Natives' Land Act. We made no promises, as previous requests for such permission had been invariably ignored. But we hoped that the Government Secretary's meeting with the sufferers and speaking with them face to face would soften the implacable red-tape and official circumlocution, and perhaps even open the way towards a modification of the administration of this legislative atrocity; but we were mistaken.

The meeting duly took place on Friday, September 12, 1913. A thousand Natives gathered at the racecourse on the wide level country between the railway station and Thaba Ncho town. A few historical facts relative to Thaba Ncho might not be out of place.

Thaba Ncho (Mount Black) takes its name from the hill below which the town is situated. Formerly this part of Africa was peopled by Bushmen and subsequently by Basutos. The Barolong, a section of the Bechuana, came here from Motlhanapitse, a place in the Western "Free" State, to which place they had been driven by Mzilikasi's hordes from over the Vaal in the early 'twenties. The Barolongs settled in Thaba Ncho during the early 'thirties under an agreement with Chief Mosheshe. The Seleka branch of the Barolong nation, under Chief Moroka, after settling here, befriended the immigrant Boers who were on their way to the north country from the south and from Natal during the 'thirties. A party of immigrant Boers had an encounter with Mzilikasi's forces of Matabele. Up in Bechuanaland the powerful Matabele had scattered the other Barolong tribes and forced them to move south and join their brethren under Moroka. Thus during the 'thirties circumstances had formed a bond of sympathy between the Boers and Barolongs in their mutual regard of the terrible Matabele as a common foe.

But the story of the relations between the Boers and the Barolong needs no comment: it is consistent with the general policy of the Boers, which, as far as Natives are concerned, draws no distinction between friend and foe. It was thus that Hendrik Potgieter's Voortrekkers forsook the more equitable laws of Cape Colony, particularly that relating to the emancipation of the slaves, and journeyed north to establish a social condition in the interior under which they might enslave the Natives without British interference. The fact that Great Britain gave monetary compensation for the liberated slaves did not apparently assuage their strong feelings on the subject of slavery; hence they were anxious to get beyond the hateful reach of British sway. They were sweeping through the country with their wagons, their families, their cattle, and their other belongings, when in the course of their march, Potgieter met the Matabele far away in the Northern Free State near a place called Vecht-kop. The trekkers made use of their firearms, but this did not prevent them from being severely punished by the Matabeles, who marched off with their horses and live stock and left the Boers in a hopeless condition, with their families still exposed to further attacks. Potgieter sent back word to Chief Moroka asking for assistance, and it was immediately granted.

Chief Moroka made a general collection of draught oxen from amongst his tribe, and these with a party of Barolong warriors were sent to the relief of the defeated Boers, and to bring them back to a place of safety behind Thaba Ncho Hill, a regular refugee camp, which the Boers named "Moroka's Hoek". But the wayfarers were now threatened with starvation; and as they were guests of honour amongst his people, the Chief Moroka made a second collection of cattle, and the Barolong responded with unheard-of liberality. Enough milch cows, and sheep, and goats were thus obtained for a liberal distribution among the Boer families, who, compared with the large numbers of their hospitable hosts, were relatively few. Hides and skins were also collected from the tribesmen, and their tanners were set to work to assist in making veldschoens (shoes), velbroeks (skin trousers), and karosses (sheepskin rugs) for the tattered and footsore Boers and their children. The oxen which they received at Vechtkop they were allowed to keep, and these came in very handy for ploughing and transport purposes. No doubt the Rev. Mr. Archbell, the Wesleyan Methodist missionary and apostle to the Barolong, played an active part on the Barolong Relief Committee, and, at that time, there were no more grateful people on earth than Hendrik Potgieter and his party of stricken voortrekkers.

After a rest of many moons and communicating with friends at Cape Colony and Natal, the Dutch leader held a council of war with the Barolong chiefs. He asked them to reinforce his punitive expedition against the Matabele. Of course they were to use their own materials and munitions and, as a reward, they were to retain whatever stock they might capture from the Matabele; but the Barolongs did not quite like the terms. Tauana especially told Potgieter that he himself was a refugee in the land of his brother Moroka. His country was Bechuanaland, and he could only accompany the expedition on condition that the Matabele stronghold at Coenyane (now Western Transvaal) be smashed up, Mzilikasi driven from the neighbourhood and the Barolong returned to their homes in the land of the Bechuana, the Boers themselves retaining the country to the east and the south (now the "Free" State and the Transvaal). That this could be done Tauana had no doubt, for since they came to Thaba Ncho, the Barolong had acquired the use of firearms — long-range weapons — which were still unknown to the Matabele, who only used hand spears. This was agreed to, and a vow was made accordingly. To make assurance doubly sure, Tauana sent his son Motshegare to enlist the co-operation of a Griqua by the name of Pieter Dout, who also had a bone to pick with the Matabele.

Pieter Dout consented, and joined the expedition with a number of mounted men, and for the time being the Boer-Barolong-Griqua combination proved a happy one. The expedition was successful beyond the most sanguine expectations of its promoters. The Matabele were routed, and King Mzilikasi was driven north, where he founded the kingdom of Matabeleland — now Southern Rhodesia — having left the allies to share his old haunts in the south.

This successful expedition was the immediate outcome of the friendly alliance between the Boers in the "Free" State and Moroka's Barolong at Thaba Ncho. But Boers make bad neighbours in Africa, and, on that account, the Government of the "Free" State thereafter proved a continual menace and hostile inroads constantly engineered against the Basuto for purposes of aggression, and the friendliness of the Barolong was frequently exploited by the Boers in their raids, undertaken to drive the Basuto further back into the mountains. This, however, must be said to the honour of the mid-nineteenth century "Free" Staters, in contrast to the "Free" Staters of later date: that the earlier "Free" Staters rewarded the loyalty of their Barolong allies by recognizing and respecting Thaba Ncho as a friendly native State; but it must also be stated that the bargain was all in the favour of one side; thereby all the land captured from the Basuto was annexed to the "Free" State, while the dusky warriors of Moroka, who bore the brunt of the battles, got nothing for their pains. So much was this the case that Thaba Ncho, which formerly lay between the "Free" State and Basutoland, was subsequently entirely surrounded by "Free" State territory.

Eventually Chief Moroka died, and a dispute ensued between his sons concerning the chieftainship. Some Boers took sides in this dispute and accentuated the differences. In 1884, Chief Tsipinare, Moroka's successor, was murdered after a night attack by followers of his brother Samuel, assisted by a party of "Free" State Boers. It is definitely stated that the unfortunate chief valiantly defended himself. He kept his assailants at bay for the best part of the day by shooting at them through the windows of his house, which they had surrounded; and it was only by setting fire to the house that they managed to get the chief out, and shoot him. As a matter of fact the house was set on fire by the advice of one of the Boers, and it is said that it was a bullet from the rifle of one of these Boers that killed Chief Tsipinare.

President Brand, the faithful ally of the dead chieftain, called out the burghers who reached Thaba Ncho after the strife was over. He annexed Thaba Ncho to the "Free" State, and banished the rival chief from "Free" State territory, with all his followers. The Dutch members of the party which assassinated the chief were put upon a kind of trial, and discharged by a white jury at Bloemfontein.

Of course, Boers could not be expected to participate in any adventure which did not immediately lead to land grabbing. But, fortunately for some Barolongs, the dead chief had in his lifetime surveyed some farms and granted freehold title to some of the tribesmen. In fact, his death took place while he was engaged in that democratic undertaking. The Boer Government, which annexed the territory, confiscated all the land not yet surveyed, and passed a law to the effect that those Barolongs who held individual title to land could only sell their farms to white people. It must, however, be added that successive Boer Presidents have always granted written exemptions from this drastic measure. So that any Native who wanted to buy a farm could always do so by applying for the President's permission, while, of course, no permission was necessary to sell to a white man; several Natives, to the author's knowledge, have thus bought farms from Natives, and also from white men, by permission of the State President, and the severity of the prohibition was never felt. But after the British occupation in 1900, the Natives keenly felt this measure, as the Governor, when appealed to by a Native for permission to buy a farm, always replied that he had no power to break the law. Thus, under the Union Jack, sales have gone on from black to white, but none from white to black, or even from black to black. In the crowd which met Mr. Dower that morning were two Barolong young men who had lately inherited a farm each under the will of their deceased uncle, and the law will not permit the Registrar of Deeds to give them title to their inheritance; their numerous representations to the Union authorities have only met with promises, while lawyers have taken advantage of the hitch to mulct them in more money than the land is worth. The best legal advice they have received is that they should sell their inheritances to white men. Now the Natives' Land Act, as applied to the whole Union of South Africa, is modelled on these highly unsatisfactory conditions relating to land in the "Free" State. The six months' imprisonment, the 100 Pounds fine, and other penalties for infringement of the Land Act, are borrowed from Chapter XXXIV of the "Free" State laws, to which reference is made in Section 7 of the Natives' Land Act. Section 8 of the Natives' Land Act is a re-enactment of some of the reprehensible "Free" State land laws which had been repealed by the Crown Colony Government after the British occupation in 1900. When the Natives' Land Bill was before Parliament the Opposition moved that the remaining native farms be scheduled as a native area, where Natives might purchase farms, of course from other Natives. The passage of such an amendment was more than could be expected as the real object of the Natives' Land Bill was to block every possible means whereby a Native may acquire land from a Native, or from any one else; but when the motion was rejected the Natives of Thaba Ncho were exceedingly alarmed. They telegraphed their fears to Mr. Sauer, who promised to visit them when Parliament rose, but his purpose was frustrated by his death, immediately after the passage of the Act.

To return to Mr. Dower's meeting, the Native Affairs Secretary received a warm welcome from the Natives, who hoped that his coming would show them a way out of their dilemma. As already stated, a thousand Natives came from the surrounding farms, some on horseback, others on bicycles, and other conveyances such as carts, wagons, *etc.*; they included evicted wanderers and native tenants under notice to leave their farms, with letters of eviction and other evidence in their pockets; they included some refugees, who had likewise been evicted from other districts — refugees who, as one of them put it, were "constantly on the move, and hurried hither to plead for shelter for our homeless families, now living in wagons."

The morning was showery. Thaba Ncho Hill in the background, always visible for scores of miles in every direction, towered high above the surrounding landscape. Its stony slopes covered with a light mist from peak to base, it stood like a silent witness to the outraged treaty between the Barolong and the Boers.

Mr. Dower, who was accompanied by his secretary (Mr. Apthorpe) and the Thaba Ncho Magistrate (Major Robertson) and the Location Superintendent, addressed the Natives for half an hour. The speeches were correctly interpreted by Mr. Jeremiah Makgothi, a native farmer, and formerly a local school teacher, who collaborated with Canon Crisp in the translation of the Scriptures into Serolong for the world-renowned S.P.C.K. The Rev. P. K. Motiyane, the local Wesleyan minister, also assisted in the task of interpretation.

Mr. Dower made some pathetic references to the life and work of the late Hon. J. W. Sauer, the great Cape politician who had just passed away; then he proceeded to refer at length to sundry inconsequential topics of minor local significance; and, having repeated his great pleasure at seeing them, without making a single reference to the momentous measure that was ravaging the Natives of the country, the Government Secretary resumed his seat amidst looks of astonishment and consternation from the assembled Natives.

The Rev. J. D. Goronyane, a gentleman who, as secretary to the late chiefs, played a leading part in the Boer-Barolong relations of the nineteenth century, was the next speaker. He thanked the Secretary for coming. No people, he said, regretted Mr. Sauer's death more than the Barolong; they had looked forward to meeting him in connexion with the new cloud now looming over the country in the shape of the Land Act, and they were sorry that his coming had been frustrated by a Higher Power. Turning to Mr. Dower, he said: "All the people you see before you are frightened by the new law. They have come here for nothing else but to hear how they are expected to live under it."

Other speakers followed, but when the actual sufferers began to narrate their experiences there were so many who wished to come forward that the leaders decided that, their cases being more or less similar, they should wait and hear how the representative of the Government would deal with the cases of those who had already spoken.

==

Mr. Dower's reply

He regretted that, as one speaker had said, some people read the Act through the spectacles coloured by their desires. Others seemed to be glad at the uncertainty and endeavoured to keep on turning the wheel of discontent. It was true that some people were imposing on the Natives, but, on the whole, there was a reasonable desire to comply with the Act, although it was not always properly understood. Few individuals had been evicted, though many had received notice. Some of the notices given under a misapprehension, and with a desire not to contravene the Act, had, since the Magistrates' explanations, actually been withdrawn. "So your best course is to explain the facts to your Magistrates, if possible, in the presence of the master." (A Voice: "Who'll bring him there?") After explaining that the principle of the Act was a first step towards territorial segregation, Mr. Dower said it gave protection to some parts of the country which formerly were not so protected. He mentioned as an instance that more than one-half of the farms formerly owned by Natives in that district were no longer in their possession. In other Provinces *the act was restrictive*, while *in the free state it was prohibitive*. The old practice of "sowing on the halves" might continue so long as the lawfully executed contracts lasted; but at the expiration of those contracts the practice should cease, as Parliament had decided on its abolition. It amounted to a partnership between a white man and a black man. With a civilized Native the system might have been good, but a raw Native always got the worst of the partnership. He would advise them to make the best temporary arrangements within the four corners of the law. It might be by adopting one of three alternatives: (1) Become servants (in which case it would be legal for a master to give them pieces of land to plough and graze a number of stock); or (2) move into the reserve — (voices: "Where is the reserve?"); or (3) dispose of the stock for cash. (Sensation.) The arrangement would only be temporary until Parliament took further steps in terms of the Commission's report. It would be better than trekking from pillar to post, till all the cattle had died out, and eventually returning penniless. Farmers always had the right to evict their native tenants. (A voice: "But we could go elsewhere.") Because some old laws which had been repealed had now been re-enacted, let them not think that there was a desire to oppress. "They may have been unjust, as you say, but understand that this law is not the last thing said by Parliament. A final settlement must depend on the recommendations of the Commission, and such action will be taken as will be to the lasting interests of white and black. The Lands Commission has already held its first sitting, and you will be serving your best interests by bringing all your information to the Magistrate, so that it be laid before the Commission. Show by your wise action that you are inspired by the justice of your case. The course of agitation will not help you. Remove suspicions and mistrust from your minds, and bring cases of real hardships to the Magistrate, who will see that this Act is administered as smoothly as possible. But *the act does not provide for any special cases in the free state* being submitted to the Governor-General under the first section of the Act." ==

The concluding statement settled the minds of those who had expected from the Government any protection against the law, and the disappointment under which the meeting broke up was indescribable. This law is full of rude shocks, and this day this spokesman of the Government told the Natives that in the other three Provinces the Governor-General will only exercise his right in exceptional cases, while in the "Free" State the law did not permit him to exercise it even in such cases, so that the Government alone knows why that provision was inserted.

Chapter IX The Fateful 13

> He hath disgraced me and laughed at my losses, mocked at my gains,
>   scorned my nation, thwarted my bargains, cooled my friends,
>   heated mine enemies; and what is his reason? I am a Kafir.
> Hath not a Kafir eyes? hath not a Kafir hands, organs, dimensions,
>   senses, affections, passions? Is he not fed with the same food,
>   hurt with the same weapons, subject to the same diseases,
>   healed by the same means, warmed and cooled by the same summer and winter
>   as a white Afrikander?
> If you prick us, do we not bleed? If you tickle us, do we not laugh?
> If you poison us, do we not die? And if you wrong us,
>   shall we not revenge? If we are like you in the rest,
>   we will resemble you in that.
> Merchant of Venice.

The Natives of South Africa, generally speaking, are intensely superstitious. The fact that they are more impressionable than tractable causes them, it seems, to take naturally to religion, and seems a flat contradiction of Junius's assertion that "there are proselytes from atheism, but none from superstition." With some South African tribes it is unlucky to include goats amongst the animals paid by a young man's parents as the dowry for his bride; it was equally bad to pay dowry in odd numbers of cattle. The payment must be made in an even number of oxen, sheep, or other animals or articles, such as two, four, six, eight, ten, and so on. The man who could not afford more than one sheep to seal the marriage contract would have to exchange his goat for a sheep to make up a presentable pair. If he were too poor to do that, a needle or any other article was admissible to make up the dowry to an even number, and so avoid giving one or three, or more odd numbers of articles. Conscious as they were of the existence of some Supreme Being, but worshipping no God, true or false, the white man's religion which makes such a worship obligatory through a mediator found easy access among so susceptible a people; and with equal ease they likewise adopted the civilization of the white man. But the Natives received not only the white man's civilization and his religion, but have even gullibly imbibed his superstitions. Thus is their dread of the figure 13 accounted for. The Native witch-doctors in the early days took advantage of their credulity, whilst civilized people traded on their susceptibilities, and the semi-civilized Natives also traded upon the fears of their more impressionable brethren.

To give a concrete case or two, we might say that when the main reservoir of the Kimberley waterworks was built, one of the labourers one week-end lost the whole of his weekly pay. He inquired, and searched everywhere he could think of, but nobody had seen his missing purse. But on Monday morning he conceived a plan for the recovery of his lost purse. In pursuance of this plan, on the Monday he asked for and obtained a day off; then he declared to the gang of labourers that he was going to the nearest location to consult a bone-thrower. Instead of going to the location, however, he went to the open country, gathered some plants, returned to the dormitories while the others were at work, boiled the herbs in a pot of water and put it aside to cool. When the workmen returned for their midday meal he announced an imaginary consultation he had had with the bone-thrower, and that that functionary had divined the whereabouts of the purse; it was to the effect that the purse had been stolen and was in the possession of a fellow-worker. "The doctor," he said, "gave me some herbs. I have cooked them, and by his direction each of you is invited to immerse his hands in the decoction which is now cool. If you are not the thief, nothing would happen to you, but to the one who has stolen my money," he added with emphasis, "the doctor said that the medicine will snap the thief's fingers clean off and leave him only with the palm."

One by one the men dipped their hands in the "medicine", and as they took turns at the pot, one young fellow at length became visibly disturbed, and believing that the concoction was true, he confessed to the theft and undertook to refund the money, rather than lose his fingers.

Another case was this. "A Transkeian missionary once heard of the serious indisposition of a Native. It was not a natural sickness, it was believed, but was the effect of sorcery, and news in that sense was noised abroad. Such cases primitive Natives believe to be beyond the skill of a medical man. White doctors, they would say, know next to nothing at all about such things. They do not believe in witchcraft and how could they be expected to be able to smell it out of a patient. Only a witch-doctor — if he is more skilful — can smell out and subdue the charm directed by another witch-doctor into the body of the bewitched.

Having heard this piece of native philosophy on witchcraft, the missionary startled the Natives by telling them in their own tongue that he could cure the disease. And he did cure it. He captured a baby lizard from the rocks which abound in the craggy undulations of most parts of the Transkei. He hid it in the inside pocket of his coat and proceeded to the sick-bed with some real medicines in his hand. "When a man who is not sick imagines himself sick," says Dr. Kellogg, "he must be sick indeed," and truly, in accordance with this saying, the Native was dangerously ill. A bone-thrower, who had in the presence and hearing of the sick man divined his malady, pronounced that he was not only bewitched by a snake, but also that the reptile was within him and was eating him to death. In these circumstances the missionary administered an emetic to the reluctant patient, in the presence of some incredulous spectators, who had never known a white man to extract a reptile from the person of a bewitched Native. Further, by some agility of the hand, the missionary produced from his pocket unobserved, just as the emetic was acting, the baby lizard he had taken from the rocks. So smartly was this done that everybody, including the patient, believed the reptile to have been extracted from his body by the power of the medicine administered by the missionary. The sick man at once stood up and walked, and the missionary was known, by all who witnessed the marvel, as the greatest witch-doctor of the neighbourhood.

In like manner, when some civilized Christians made remarks on New Year's Day about the figure 13, there was much gossiping among the more superstitious Natives as to the form of trouble which the year 1913 had in store for the Natives, although none knew that a revolutionary law of Draconian severity would be launched in their midst during this eventful year.

The powerful African potentate, Menelik of Abyssinia (whose death had been falsely circulated no fewer than seven times during the past dozen years), really died in 1913.

Letsie *ii*, paramount chief of the semi-independent Basuto nation, departed this life during this same year.

Dinizulu (son of the great Cetewayo, whose impis slew the Prince Imperial in 1879), who was born to inherit the throne of his fathers, and who lived to be one of the most disappointed men of his day, spent many years in prison and in exile, and was known in his lifetime as the Black Napoleon; was released from prison by the Union Government, and given back his pension of 500 Pounds per annum. Sharing the hopes of his people that in accordance with the Government's erstwhile good intentions now tottering before a growing Republicanism, Zululand would be restored to the Zulus, and he established as their ruler under the Crown. He, too, died in the year 1913.

An unusually large number of good and noble men of greater or lesser renown were gathered to their fathers during this year.

It is perhaps not generally known that few British statesmen did so much for the South African Natives, in so short a term of service at the Colonial Office, as the Hon. A. Lyttleton. And he, too, left us rather suddenly during this troublous year of 1913. In this year, too, South Africa was visited by a drought which for severity was pronounced to be unprecedented in the knowledge of all the old inhabitants. Remarks — some pithy, some ugly — were made upon the drought by Dutchmen. They all remembered how the God of their fathers used to send them nice soaking rains regularly each spring-time, and that it usually continued to nourish the plants and other of the country's vegetation throughout the summer, and they concluded that there must be some reason why He does not do it now. The majority of Dutchmen whom the writer thus overheard attributed the visitation to the sins of the foreigners, who are fast buying up the country, and cursing it by settling godless people upon it. One or two saw in it the vengeance of the Supreme Being for the unnecessary persecution of His black creatures, but they were afraid to say this aloud. "See," said one, "is the drought not worse in the `Free' State where Kafirs seem to be very hard hit by this new law?" This was true. Dutchmen's cattle were dying of poverty in the "Free" State, and the land was so parched in some parts that it seemed difficult to believe that grass could ever grow in these places again, supposing the long-looked-for rain came at last.

On our birthday, October 9, 1913, they hanged four murderers who had been condemned to death at the preceding criminal sessions. The selection of the morning of our birthday for the execution of four prisoners at our home was curious as executions in Kimberley take place only about once or twice in ten years. The event, of course, was purely accidental; but middle-aged Natives seemed to have an aptitude for remembering catastrophes which, in the lives of their fathers and their fathers' fathers, followed such coincidences. Whilst the executions were taking place, on the morning of our birthday, an ugly ocean tragedy was taking place away out on the Atlantic. The `Vulturno' was ablaze with a number of passengers on board. Innocent white men and women were being roasted alive, because the sea was too rough to permit their transfer from the burning ship to the rescuing liners; and so they perished, literally, "between the devil and the deep sea" — within full view of relief.

Dutchmen as a rule are like Natives in that they live as long as they can, and die only when they must; but in the Transvaal a Dutch farmer all but exterminated his family on this day with a revolver, which he had previously secured for the purpose. On this day also the mind of an English miner at Randfontein having suddenly become unhinged, he shot his wife, his baby, and his aunt, then coolly pocketing the pistol, he cycled down to the school, called out his two children, shot them down in cold blood, and retired to a quiet place where he put an end to his own life. During that fateful week in which disaster followed disaster in rapid succession, there occurred the following, namely, the colliery disaster at Cardiff, which left a thousand dependents without breadwinners, to say nothing of the damage to property, which is estimated at over 100,000 Pounds. There were also railway accidents and aviation disasters, causing damage to life and property. There were commercial troubles due to the Johannesburg strike in July, and this effect of the strike indicates the influence exercised by the "golden city" over South African commerce. In that sad upheaval in the labour world many innocent people lost their lives and property, and unfortunately, as is always the case, besides adding largely to the taxpayers' burdens, seriously affected people who had nothing to do with the strike. Yet when some of our friends expressed thankfulness that the year did not have thirteen months, we were obstinate enough to refuse to waste valuable time in considering the subject.

Individuals, like communities, suffered heavily from one cause or another in the year 1913. Thus the writer's little family also had its baptism of sorrow. On New Year's Day of that year 1913, his little boy, a robust child of three months, was prattling in the house. He first saw the light in the last quarter of 1912, on the very day we opened and christened our printing office, so we named him after

Printed in Great Britain
by Amazon